Considering Computer Contracting?

Considering Computer Contracting?

MICHAEL POWELL

BUTTERWORTH
HEINEMANN

OXFORD AUCKLAND BOSTON JOHANNESBURG MELBOURNE NEW DELHI

Butterworth-Heinemann
Linacre House, Jordan Hill, Oxford OX2 8DP
225 Wildwood Avenue, Woburn, MA 01801-2041
A division of Reed Educational and Professional Publishing Ltd

℞ A member of the Reed Elsevier plc group

First published 1999
© Michael Powell 1999

TRADEMARKS/REGISTERED TRADEMARKS
Computer hardware and software brand names mentioned in this book are protected by their respective trademarks and are acknowledged.

British Library Cataloguing in Publication Data
A catalogue record for this book is available from the British Library

ISBN 0 7506 3851 6

Typeset by P.K.McBride, Southampton
Printed and bound in Great Britain

Contents

About the Author

Michael Powell has worked in the computer industry since leaving Oxford University in 1970. After some years working his way through programming and systems analysis jobs, he became a contractor in 1975, before returning to full-time employment in the software industry, working for a number of software companies. He returned to contracting again in 1984 and continues to work as a freelance consultant. He has written a number of packages for clients, and for his own company, which have enjoyed considerable success in their marketplaces. He is fortunate enough to be able to work almost entirely from his office at home in a converted Cotswold farmhouse.

He combines contracting with freelance writing. However, his real love is opera singing, and contracting provides him with the right environment to enjoy this. He is a semi-professional tenor who has performed over 30 operatic roles.

He is very happily married with two grown up children of his own and two step-children. His ambition for them is that they will provide for his and his wife's old age in the fashion to which they would like to become accustomed.

Acknowledgement

I would like to make a special acknowledgement to Catherine Fear — my copy editor — who really contributed a lot of valuable ideas. Thank you very much for all your input. Much appreciated. M.P.

1 | **Introduction**

The computer industry — or more accurately the data processing industry — has become mature. Its effects are felt throughout society, and its terminology has entered into the language. The growth has been meteoric, perhaps as great as any since the Industrial Revolution. To service this new industry, a whole range of new skills has been created. Forty years ago there were no programmers, data processing systems analysts, or other computer staff in commercial employment. Even fifteen years ago, the PC was only just beginning to make itself felt, and nobody but the most optimistic would have forecast its impact on all areas of life. Now computing staff represent a sizeable and growing proportion of the workforce. The growth of the Internet and the use of e-mail represent another revolution — introducing a completely new set of media.

The effects of this growth on staffing have been immense. It has never been possible to find enough qualified personnel in this industry. Even the recessions in the industry in 1972, 1981 and the early 1990s were only relative compared to the rest of the economy. The 1990s have seen so much change that, even though some computer jobs have been lost, many more have been created. In many ways, the IT industry has led others out of recession. Because of this, demand for skills is sky-rocketing. In reality, there have been never really been problems for properly skilled staff. Moreover, the industry is still growing, and all projections for the future jobs market point to an unending need for staff. My only concern is that one day I will wake up and discover that nobody does anything except computing — and the whole of society will do a virtual oozlum bird.

Staff growth is also fuelled by the continuing changes in technology. In 1995, Microsoft was cool about the Internet. By 1997, it was completely turned around and every Microsoft product had been changed to interface with it. In version 5 of their C++ compiler, suddenly the Help files were using HTML instead of their own proprietary interface. In fact, this change was rather ill-thought-out because the HTML files were far worse cross-referenced and indexed than the normal Help files. The Internet has created the need for more and more staff — those experienced in Windows programming, those who understand HTML, Java, and ActiveX controls — not to mention Web page designers and creative artists to take maximum advantage of the new technology. Now, the latest cool stuff is the Intranet — which seems to be almost as important as the Internet, because it is seen as capable of "empowering" everybody within an organisation.

As the century draws to a close, an ominous problem has created a need for programming skills which had been thought completely obsolete. The "Millennium bug" — which, untreated, will cause many older systems to fail at the start of the twenty-first century — has been estimated to need as many programmers as the whole current population of skilled staff. Those programmers will need to know older, batch languages like COBOL and PL/I. Because of this, older programmers are being brought out of retirement and employed — some at up to £1,000 per day — to address the problem.

The other opportunity which is already creating jobs is the possible introduction of European Monetary Union (EMU). This is already — in 1998 — exercising the banks, because, if it is introduced, they will need to cater for it even if the UK does not adopt it immediately. It's pretty farcical, considering the state of the economies of the main protagonists – but all the analyses point to its being as big a potential problem for IT departments as the Millennium bug. The reasons for this are twofold. Firstly, though this might seem a trivial problem, few, if any, keyboards and fonts yet support the Euro symbol. Converting them will be a major cost. Secondly, and more important, systems which deal with monetary amounts will need to be adapted to operate in two currencies. This is not a problem for systems already handling foreign currency amounts, but domestic systems will almost certainly need to be adapted to cope. Some companies already intend to operate with the Euro alongside the Pound — even though that will not be mandatory. Anybody dealing with those companies will need to be able to cope — as will the companies themselves.

The main change which has occurred since this book was first published is to the profile of the industry. Then, mainframe sites were still a large factor, demanding a high proportion of available staff. Although the PC had made itself felt, the "downsizing" trend was still only forecast, and client-server applications an afterthought in a learned text. Nowadays the PC is king. Windows applications programming is a major growth area, and no application worth its salt is considered unless it works on a client-server platform. These skills are so new, and so little understood, that those contractors with the relevant experience in them have been able to command premium rates. Those rates are no longer so far out of line with the pay enjoyed within the employed sector, as employers desperately try to hang on to trained staff — who can almost demand their own price.

Changes continue apace. Machines which would have seemed super computers just a few years ago are now on desks which would never before have hosted anything more technical than a stapler. People who profess themselves unable to operate their microwave — let alone their video recorder — are now expected to be able to surf the Net, run spreadsheets and process their words instead of letting secretaries do it for them. Software gets ever more sophisticated. A word processor now takes 100 Megabytes of disk space, while its predecessors, a decade ago, were delivered on a handful of low density diskettes. It has built-in programming languages, and does far more than ever before. But, in the main, these functions are largely unused — and the ones that may be useful sometimes have dubious worth. Microsoft's standard Office97 dictionary says that the word "liaise" should be spelt "liase" (I know because I am looking at this document with Word97 and the former — correct — spelling has been underlined in red, while the latter has not, and that spelling is suggested if I check the word). There's so much spare processing capacity in today's behemoth machines that your word processor can run a dancing paperclip of all things! It is looking quizzically at me even as I type — no, I don't need a hint from you!

All this has meant that the chronic shortage of staff in the industry — which has only dipped a little during the worst of recessions over the last thirty years — continues. The opportunities for competent qualified staff are better than they have ever been, and there's no end in sight.

The type of contract work available has been changing, too. In the bad old days, contractors were a minority. They were considered outside the norm. Today, more and more jobs are contracted out — even milkmen have been given self-employed contracts. This means that the status of the contractor is much more acceptable than it was a few years ago. A contractor is no longer the lone wolf among a group of staff. In many places the majority of the workforce are contractors — many of them ex-employees of the company taking their first independent steps.

Contracting is not everybody's cup of tea. For those who crave a sense of belonging to an organisation, or who feel the need of security, a full-time job may be far more appropriate. This security issue is more perceived than actual. Indeed, contracting is often more secure than full-time working. However, there is no question that, when it comes to such necessities as raising a mortgage, sorting out tax affairs and dealing with pensions, contractors have to do more work than their full-time colleagues.

Contracting seldom brings status. It is extremely unlikely that a company will subcontract a genuine management task, for instance. They might bring in a management consultant — but that is a different matter. If status matters, contracting may not be for you.

In some industries, going freelance involves a major step — one that you would want to discuss with your family before taking, because of the possible detrimental effect on your finances before you start to earn a living. A spouse's income can be important to support you through the lean times — as a freelance singer and journalist, I know these periods only too well! However, the contracting marketplace remains so buoyant that you are probably, if anything, more secure as a freelance than as a full-timer. This might change, but, if it does, it seems very unlikely that most full-time jobs will offer any more security — because the economy will be in deep recession.

However, there is one eventuality which can affect your ability to earn — and here you will be in a worse position than your full-time friends. If you become ill, you will have to cope with that on your own, without the benefit of sick pay from your employer. This problem may not be quite so bad, though, if you are able to work from home. I have been able to work in my office at home while suffering from a bad back, or a fluey cold which would have forced me to take a day off if I had had to commute.

Often the contractor will be resented by full-time employees. Their rates of pay make them look very affluent in comparison to those who, for their part, have protection of employment, pensionability and other fringe benefits — but can seldom run to the BMW or Jaguar. Nonetheless, staff are becoming more resigned to this nowadays, and often make the choice of remaining full-time employees rather than contracting, to preserve their fringe benefits and chosen career path. It is also true that, in surveys, the most-quoted next step for contractors is back into employment.

Contractors have traditionally been an odd breed. They are often more experienced than the average for the level of work which they are doing. They should not have the same desire to belong which gives to others a sense of security, and they should not desire or require too much job satisfaction. Often, but not always, an overriding motivation is money. However there are a number of other reasons for being self-employed, of a rather worthier kind.

I am a case in point. I have three jobs. Apart from contracting, I write, and I sing professionally. This last job does not earn me any real money – indeed, when I compare my earnings to my expenditure on travel , singing lessons and coaching and music, I definitely make a loss. However, it is an important part of my life – and one which contracting enables me to pursue. Because I work from home – so seldom have to waste time travelling to and from work – I am able to balance my time between my occupations. I can work at night on my singing and contract during the day. When I am rehearsing for a production, I can attend during the day and contract at night. As long as I deliver the goods – and I have an excellent and understanding client – it does not matter what working pattern I adopt – and during any spare time I have, I can do some writing. Contracting makes all this possible.

This book will explore many aspects of the contracting world, and attempt to give advice to both the newcomer and the experienced contractor, as well as to those employers wrestling with the perennial problem of finding staff in this highly competitive marketplace.

We will be looking at why contract workers are used at all – what kind of companies actually employ contractors, and why? How do you make the transition from full-time working – what does it actually take temperamentally to be a successful contractor? How do you start – what does forming your own company involve, and why is it even necessary? How do you go about finding a contract, and negotiating the right rate? What do agencies do for you – and how can you find who are the best? What are the financial differences between being a full-time employee, and a contractor – how do you manage your affairs? How can you keep your experience up-to-date when you do not have a regular employer to help train you? What sort of opportunities are available, and what sort of rates of pay can you expect? Lastly, we will explore your possible career progressions after contracting.

This latest edition will explore the current areas for opportunity which have opened and those which have declined. The changing scene, while closing some doors, has opened many others. Indeed, it is a great surprise to many of us old fogies to see companies which had assumed that we were past it coming back — not exactly cap in hand — to beg for those outdated ("legacy") skills like Cobol to help them solve those niggly little Millennium problems so conveniently ignored in the past.

It's a great time to be a contractor.

2 | Who uses contractors and why?

In the June 1995 edition of the *Director* magazine there was an article ("Valiant knight seeks short-term contract") in which Charles Handy analysed the increasing trend towards task-centred work, forecasting that we would soon see companies as collections of medium-term projects, co-ordinated by other medium-term groups. He also quoted the astonishing figure of only 55 per cent of the available workforce being in full-time jobs — a figure declining year by year. All studies since that time have shown the trend continuing. The contractor is therefore becoming more and more common.

On the face of it, you might find it hard to see why companies should need to take on contract workers. There is a perception that they are more expensive to use, do not generally feel company loyalty, and that they cannot be governed and controlled like full-time staff. It would seem to be far more economical to employ people directly, cut out the agency middle man, and avoid possible difficulties with normal employment and taxation legislation.

However, in the IT industry, not only is the demand for such people buoyant, but it is growing steadily with no end in sight. There are a number of reasons for this, which will be explored in this chapter. Moreover, the trend towards task- or project-centred working brings with it the need for shorter term contractual arrangements.

2.1 Why do companies take on contract staff?

Updating old systems

The most obvious area where a contractor can be useful is to counteract a shortage of specific skills within the computer department. For instance, a company may have bought a computer some years ago from a supplier who provided a "solution" (hardware and software together). The computer is now out of date but still functional. The company has now decided to implement a new system, and wishes to use its own resources, because the software house has moved on, and no longer writes new systems for that machine. The company decides therefore to write the programs in-house. However, there are no computing staff within the company, and there is no intention to build up a department.

The solution then is to find development staff, managed by the company, but on a relatively short-term basis, to implement the system. It is quite likely that, even if the company wanted to find suitable permanent staff, they would not succeed. Not many DP people want to become bogged down in old-fashioned technology. However, freelancers are prepared to do this, if they are offered a sufficient incentive, and will not be required to do the work for a long period.

As we discussed in the opening chapter, the "Millennium bug" has introduced a new requirement. "legacy systems" — those written in the 1960s and 1970s for mainframes and early mini-computers — were only expected to have a limited lifespan. The consensus of opinion was that such systems would not need to last for more than a few years before being superseded. Those estimates did not take account of how well-written such systems were, and, twenty or more years on, they were still functioning.

The Millennium bug arises from the fact that many of those systems stored dates in the form "YYMMDD" — often as packed decimal numbers. This saved space and seemed fine at the time. The reason for storing in that order is to be able to sort on date. When we get to 2000, the year will become "00". As a result, the system will misinterpret them in two ways. Firstly it will sort them to the wrong end of a list — so possibly processing them in the wrong sequence. For instance, an invoice raised at the end of 1999 might have a payment which the system would interpret as happening before the invoice. Secondly, many systems will merely add "19" to the year to get the correct date. In that case, all those records will be interpreted as being 100 years old. It does not take a genius to see the possible implications as customers are sent automatic court summonses for being a century in arrears!

There are other Millennium bugs — one which is due to happen sooner is the GPS bug. All the satellite-based systems which help guide ships and planes to their destination (Global Positioning Systems) use a clock to determine their latitude and longitude. This was based originally on a number of weeks from a set date. That number of weeks was held in a 10-bit number — 1024 weeks in all. The initial reference date was in the late 1970s — so the older GPS systems will all fail in August 1998. We are assured that this will not happen — that all modern machines are corrected. But I'm not sure I want to be flying that week.

The other Millennium bug is that which will affect older PCs. In earlier versions of the BIOS, these machines did not allow for the Millennium — and systems using this version will fail in 2000. Microsoft have a fix, which allows the problem to be bypassed in software, but a machine which needs it should be treated with circumspection. It is relatively easy to check your machine — there are a number of programs available on the Web for this. A simple pair of checks is to set the computer's clock to 23:59:00 on 31/12/1999 and then leave it running for over a minute. If the date then correctly goes to 01/01/2000, that test is passed. The other check is to set it to 23:59:00 on 28/02/2000. If the date, after a minute has passed, shows as 29/02/2000, the BIOS programming is correct (every century is not a leap year — despite being divisible by 4 — except every four centuries). If it shows as 01/03/2000, the computer is faulty.

There is, built into Microsoft's own most up-to-date C++ classes (in version 5), another Millennium bug, which will happen in 2038. If you use the "CTime" or "CDate" class in your programs, the date must lie between 1970 and 2038 (for some quite inexplicable reason). This can be overridden by not using those classes (or overriding the standard code in them) — and you must do that to record, for instance, birth date information for people older than 27 in 1997. However, there will be people who do not realise this limitation is there and, if their systems are still in use when dates after 2038 are needed (and the obvious one is a pension or life assurance expiry date for somebody born in the late 1960s, so this could be happening sooner than Microsoft realise). I know whereof I speak because I could not extract time fields stored in a Microsoft SQL-Server database — they came out at zero because they are stored as date/time and the date is set to 1/1/1901. Because it is before 1970, the time is set to zero. Not terribly clever of Microsoft.

Supplementing in-house staff

Another allied reason is to enable a company to find better quality staff with more experience than can readily be found because there is a lack of skills on market. For example, there is always demand for IBM CICS systems programmers — indeed for systems programmers in general. Because of the complexity of their task, and the experience needed to do it, they can demand a very high price. Bringing in contractors, on a "when needed" basis, can solve the support problem, and also save money, since the work will be done better than it would by less experienced staff. Indeed, there may be no option but to use a contractor.

This way of buying in highly skilled staff is often far more economical for companies which cannot command sufficiently large budgets to enable them constantly to employ such people. But there may be a more important spin-off benefit. Contract staff, because they will move jobs more frequently than full-time employees, often have more widespread, as well as more up-to-date skills. Indeed, it may be to a company's advantage to make use of contract staff in rapidly changing areas, merely to acquire their knowledge of the very latest advances in technology. This applies in a number of areas such as structured design, database, operating system and teleprocessing, expert systems, networking and micro computer technology.

In some areas it is virtually impossible to get hold of people with particular skills — and to hold on to them if you train existing staff members. The skills which have recently fallen into this category are such things as SAP, Lotus Notes and Windows/NT. The demand in the market is so high that the only way to find qualified people is to import them as contractors.

Conversions

These are nearly always short-term, transient projects. For instance, conversions of machine or operating system require that the current system continues in operation while the new one is being developed. This will generally mean that there will be a need, for a time, for parallel teams on the two systems — one to maintain the old, the other to implement and test the new. This is an ideal area for contract staff. Unless a data processing manager wishes to build up an unnecessarily large department, which will have to be shed or redeployed later, contractors can fill the gap until all new systems are fully operational.

One area which used to be a perennial earner in the IBM mainframe environment, for instance, was DOS to OS conversions. As long ago as 1974 this was a popular sport. One contract, for a large electronics company, employed a team of around a dozen programmers, with a project leader — also a contractor — reporting to full-time management. Such arrangements still occur today, as IBM mainframe users downsize their systems. There is a lot of work involved in moving from the older proprietary systems to a Unix based client-server platform.

This sort of move involves a whole raft of new skills, such as knowledge of networking, GUIs and 4GLs. The latter have become a very normal way to produce new systems, since they provide a platform on which a development can proceed without worrying over-much about the underlying interfacing problems.

Very often, in this type of project, a database management system and/or data dictionary (DBMS/DD), such as Oracle, Microsoft's SQL Server or Sybase, is being introduced at the same time. In this case, it is frequently desirable to bring in contract staff to do the initial work, and pass on their knowledge of the new product to existing permanent personnel. In this way, many of the problems associated with learning new techniques can easily be overcome. It is usually far cheaper to train people by getting their hands dirty than by theoretical courses, as long there are suitably knowledgeable experts to turn to. This is one of the richest areas of contracting skill, and has been for some years.

Tools such as Uniface and PowerBuilder, which can support many DBMS and GUI environments virtually transparently, are being used to create some very complex software. Knowledge of these products gives a programmer a very powerful niche to exploit. Very often the experienced contractor will start the ball rolling on a new product or tool, then hand over to an in-house team which he or she has trained. However, some companies nowadays employ contractors exclusively to develop the use of particular tools, and let their in-house staff do more conventional work.

It is interesting to see the agencies in action in this case. When a large organisation is looking for a particular skill, it approaches a number of agencies. Similarly, any contractor with a modicum of sense will approach more than one agency. I have quite often been called four or five times by different agencies about a particular project, for which I have a particular skill — even when I have already met the client, and been rejected (or done the rejecting — much more usual!).

Conversion work can now be a continuous money spinner in some areas, for instance, upgrading software in the Microsoft arena. First we moved to Windows 3 — a massive culture shock. Then we had Windows/NT. This was not such a big change on paper, but, to use its full 32-bit potential meant re-compiling everything, and fiddly changes to code. Then we had Windows 95. If you'd passed through to NT this was not such a problem, but Windows 3.1 to Windows 95 is a huge change. Now we have NT 4 and the rise of Internet – HTML versions of forms instead of conventional programs, and code written in Java and using ActiveX controls. It is hard even to stay conversant with the technology, let alone manage conversion — if you need to — without bringing in experts. NT 5 — though much hyped — still does not look like appearing until late in 1998, but that will bring a major change to the marketplace as the new directory services and other facilities are implemented. Microsoft would dearly love to convert all Unix systems to NT — but that is unlikely to happen for a time.

One-off projects

In any data processing environment, there is a need for one-off, non-maintained projects. These frequently arise because of extraordinary, unforeseeable reasons. One example is the year-end audit workload. Although it is usually fairly easy to predict the work which will be needed, its very nature is such that it can easily have a very bad effect on development schedules. The type of assignment is usually fairly mundane — report production, possibly using a fourth-generation language, creation of audit data files for analysis on micro spreadsheet systems, "merging" programs, to bring together branch data for head office analysis, etc. These jobs can rapidly cause disillusion and boredom within a development department — especially if staff have to be withdrawn from more interesting and exciting work. Contractors can help here — by nature they must be more flexible in the work they expect than the average programmer.

One of the dullest projects I can remember is one I had in 1995, thankfully of only 15 days duration, when I had to do Uniface programming to specification for a company in the Midlands. I had no idea of the overall system — nor time to learn it. I merely had to transcribe 4GL statements already more or less coded by the analysts. Since I did not really know what the system should do, I could do little to check whether what I was doing was correct — that was left to the analysts themselves. Quite coincidentally, I was singing in London every night, so was doing a 250-mile per day round trip. Not only was it extremely boring, but tiring too.

I was not sorry when that came to an end. It was replaced by a really sparkling job, doing analysis for a merchant bank, prior to their converting a system they had running in Switzerland. The place was a real sweatshop — a bunch of really bright people working in a poorly-cooled room full to overflowing with heat-generating equipment in the height of summer. Apart from the heat it was a wonderful environment. In contrast to the rigidity of the earlier project, it was almost completely free-form — there was not even a job specification — I had to develop it as I went along. I was really sad when personal circumstances forced me to leave that before its completion. In just six weeks I saw contracting from opposite ends of the spectrum.

Confidential work

Confidential work, such as that on company consolidations and mergers, is an area in which contractors are often used. Like audit work, this often involves creating many ad hoc reports, often of a confidential nature. Contractors — assuming that they sign necessary undertakings on confidentiality — can provide a more secure work force than in-house staff. After all, they are unlikely to "get the jitters" if the company is obviously in trouble, unless their contracts are thus in jeopardy. Also their loyalty is not directly to the company, as it is for full-time employees. The use of contractors to do confidential work is by no means unusual.

There are still government jobs out there — even Ministry of Defence jobs — which carry the full weight of confidentiality and security worthy of a Le Carré novel. MOD clearance is a good thing to get if you are hoping for one of these projects. This is awarded after suitable scrutiny, and, once you have it, you can apply for government jobs which would be denied to ordinary mortals.

Jobs not wanted by in-house staff

It is unreasonable to expect that full-time staff will happily swallow any work thrust at them. They need to be motivated because theirs is a longer term relationship with their employer than is the contractor's. That, at least is the theory, though I believe that contractors are actually often more resilient than their employed brethren.

A programmer who has been trained on advanced techniques, or using one of the trendier languages such as C++ is unlikely to be very happy to be presented with the job of doing a necessary upgrade to a piece of existing software written in COBOL or RPG. The result can be inefficient work or even the loss of a useful member of staff — often to contracting. Actually, there seem to be less of these jobs around these days. Indeed, it is often the in-house staff who end up doing the duller jobs. I would not like to suggest that this is because full-timers are less adventurous or inventive than part-timers. Often, the staff doing these jobs are either juniors — who are building up their personal expertise — or management — who are doing them because nobody else can be persuaded to.

A contractor may be used for such jobs, because they don't complain and are not so interested in career progression. This can mean that contractors end up doing far less interesting work than normal staff members. However, their careers do not develop in the same way, and their motivations are different.

Circumventing normal employment procedures

This may sound rather a strong category. However, it is not all that sinister. Under UK law, for instance, an employer is expected to have to give the same notice period as he can expect his employee to give. Normal employment contracts can be written otherwise, but they are unlikely to be sustainable if push comes to shove.

Where an employee has a contractual grievance with an employer, even during the initial two-year probationary period (during which full-employment protection is not available), he or she can go to the Advisory, Conciliation and Arbitration Service (ACAS) and receive a fair hearing. That process, which need not involve lawyers, is one which is frequently very sympathetic to an employee. The cost of using such a procedure is very small. ACAS is a government body which is set up to promote the improvement of industrial relations and to encourage the extension of collective bargaining and the development and reform of collective bargaining machinery — in short it's who you go to when you are in dispute with your employer.

Contractors, on the other hand, are bound by civil law. They do not have the normal, unwritten, rights of employment to which an employee is entitled. Therefore, if an employer wishes to agree a long-term contract, which he, but not the contractor, can break at short notice, and which might have performance guarantees built in, it will pay him to employ a contractor. The cost to the employer may be greater, but he can purchase thereby peace of mind.

This is often a prime motivator in employing contractors. In theory, at least, a contractor will be with you for the duration of the project. If he lets you down, you can go to the agency who placed him, and ask for a replacement. In other words, contractors can give employers a security of employment which ordinary workers do not.

This does not mean that employers are ruthlessly exploiting contractors. The consideration of a higher fee than would normally be earned in straight salary is an attractive offset to more onerous — but not unacceptable — contract terms. In many cases the employer is actually hamstrung by employment law. It would, for instance, be quite unreasonable to expect an employer to give an employee a year's notice period merely to ensure his or her services during a critical development phase.

Working directly with user departments

In many large companies, the data processing or information technology department is often given a company-wide mandate to perform all data processing development. Because of this, theoretically at least, the IT department must be involved in every decision to employ computers, and such use must be implemented by them. As a result, for instance, as micro computers have developed, user departments would have been unable to use them without waiting for the IT department both to sanction the use, and then to develop suitable software.

The result of such strictures is that users frequently feel that the IT department is completely blocking any progress towards office automation. Because of the scope of work undertaken by them, and the backlog of development endemic in all schedules, the chargeable cost of in-house development can be horrific. In addition, running certain systems on the company mainframe can be grotesquely expensive.

One way for harassed user departments to get around the problem is to use contractors. This is possible because, unlike full-time staff who must normally be approved by central personnel, many companies allow managers some leeway in temporary staff recruitment . In addition, micros are so cheap now that they can be slipped through as normal office equipment, rather than as computers. Therefore it is not unusual for contractors to be brought in, employed directly by user departments to modify packages or write systems. This can cause friction with the IT department, and contractors in this situation may need to be reasonably thick-skinned.

Avoiding trade union problems

An even more contentious area of working practices involves union membership — though this is not such a major area as it used to be, since the recession has finally swept away a lot of old ideas. An extreme example of this was Wapping, when the proprietors of The Times newspaper decided to move their whole operation lock, stock and barrel to a new site in the East End. Union members, who felt that they had been very unfairly dealt with, set up picket lines, and there were some very ugly incidents as employees, many of whom were contractors, ran the gauntlet of both verbal and physical abuse to get into work. The site was successfully installed and working with the help of contract staff. Certainly the working conditions imposed a considerable strain on all concerned.

Without making any judgement on this situation, or others of a more mild nature, it is clear that employers do sometimes feel the need to circumvent normal employment practices. For this reason, contractors can be useful. Although unions may feel that their members' jobs are being taken by such people, from the employers' viewpoint they are a necessary and desirable route to getting work done, and bypassing problems.

This particular motivation is far less common in this country these days. The Trade Unions have modernised and are now much more keen to be seen as partners than adversaries. However, it still applies abroad. There are firms in countries like France or Italy who have imported contractors to bypass local labour problems. It can be quite sticky — but they generally pay well.

Questionable companies

There are companies which have poor or questionable track records. Start-up businesses, or those which are not yet perceived to be stable, need staff as much as any other. The only solution in this field — which is not exactly suffering a glut of suitable people — may be to use contract staff until the company is more stable. The reason that a company can do this is that a contractor may take a greater risk — because his or her whole future is not at stake. Another, and more contentious, category is companies or organisations of dubious nature. I will not dwell any further on that.

No in-house development staff

There are companies which do not want to employ development or even data processing staff. It is becoming quite normal now even for large companies to eschew their own development teams. They bring in outside help only as and when they actually need it.

Small companies often intend to buy only a complete computer solution which can then be used by non-technical personnel. However, there are few packages which can totally fulfil the user requirement without any modification. Moreover, there are frequently peripheral needs such as the development of reports, using in-built report generators, which the user cannot readily meet. Either the user must rely on the software supplier to provide expertise, or must buy it in.

In the latter case, users are unlikely to be able to find, employ, and then keep, a full-time staff member. They can, after all, not offer any career development or promotion prospects. By definition — particularly in small companies, such people are merely low-skilled "gophers" whose only task is and will remain servicing the system. If it is superseded, the job, in all probability, will cease. The solution again is to bring in a contractor to do the work, either on a regular basis, or as and when needed.

From a software supplier's viewpoint, this can be an infernal nuisance. They wish to sell the product, and get out as soon as possible to sell to other clients. When there is a contractor there, the whole deal can be more difficult. The contractor often wants to prove that he or she is doing a useful job, and so "rides" the supplier harder than necessary. The supplier complains to the client, who often does not really understand the implications. All in all, this sort of contract can be very unsatisfactory from all sides. However, given a good software supplier, and a sensible contractor, such arrangements can work well — and even lead to contractors being used again by software suppliers.

This kind of work can even extend further, into the complete management of a data processing facility in a small company. This kind of "facilities management" is very attractive to inexperienced users. Once they have cut their teeth on their first system — managed by an expert — they can cope much better with managing subsequent projects themselves. Again, they take less of a risk by using a replaceable contractor than a full-time staff member.

Skills not available elsewhere

One area which is burgeoning is the supply of staff to work with new technologies — which are changing ever more rapidly. As our analysis of skills will show (see Chapter 8), the advent of Windows and its attendant development tools has been so rapid that there is an enormous shortage of relevant skills. Demand for C++ programmers, for instance, has grown by an amazing 320 per cent in a year. In such a market, it is obvious that such staff will almost be able to name their own price. One way in which this is almost always done is by becoming a contractor. This sort of work also leads to specialisation in contract agencies — some of whom claim to have larger numbers than others of staff with particular skills. Sometimes this is true, sometimes not. From the contractor's viewpoint, though, it does no harm to spread the word if you have those really heavily demanded skills.

It is also interesting to note what some of those rare skills are. Each month the computer press publish tables of desired skills (*Computer Weekly* has a regular column on this, for instance). Sometimes these skills are in such demand that there are not enough people to fill them — that applies at the moment to, for instance, SAP. Sometimes they are relatively obscure skills which have come to the fore because of a particular industry trend. That would apply to Lotus Notes — which is not really a programming language, but has ignited the minds of City firms because of the benefits it can deliver. Sometimes the skills are simply in a relatively small market, such as certain programming tools like the AS/400 product, Lansa.

Introduction of new technology

Another frequent requirement is to help in the introduction of new technology to a company. This is an extension of the conversion exercises discussed earlier, but applies here to more specialised skills. For example, a company may decide to introduce a new package, such as NT and SQL Server to support a particular package. The setting up of that environment may be beyond the scope of the package supplier, but the user cannot really justify acquiring the necessary in-house skills. A contractor will then frequently be used to smooth the transition, on the assumption that, once the product goes live, there will be no need for such a high level of skill. Contractors to do such work may be brought in by the package suppliers themselves.

2.2 What sort of companies use contractors?

Every company, from the largest to the smallest, may find a need for contract staff. However, the type of staff, and the kind of work undertaken may differ drastically. In this section I will look briefly at the types of companies who use contractors, and why. This may help in targeting your efforts to find yourself a suitable contract.

Mainframe IT departments

Many mainframe users bring in contractors regularly for such jobs as systems support work, installing new operating systems, overspill on systems implementation and so on. These are categories already discussed. What characterises the mainframe user though, typically, is the presence of an ordered DP or IT hierarchy. Therefore contracts within mainframe departments are often relatively low down in the reporting structure, reporting to those on the level of project leaders. There are, naturally, exceptions. For instance, when radically new software such as a DBMS is installed, a contractor may come in at the consultant or project leader level. However, in those circumstances that individual will often report to relatively low level managers, who have the task of actually managing the project team.

There are cases, however, where contractors at a senior level have considerable power. For sensitive or highly technical projects, specialists will often report directly to the data processing manager, or head of IT. Such people seldom actually have "people management" tasks — although there are times when they do. For instance, on large software engineering projects, if contractors with relevant experience are used, they may have teams of programmers reporting to them.

Downsizing is a major headache for such departments. All the familiar ways of working suddenly need replacing, and the skills to do this do not reside in-house. In that case, the only solution may be to employ contractors to handle the changeover, and train the in-house staff. Often one of the main results of such a change is the redundancy of many of the old guard. Without contractors to help, this can be a very difficult process to manage.

It is not at all unusual for those moved out in such a process to become contractors themselves, and then be employed by their previous employers at a far better rate of pay. I have seen a number of places where the contractors outnumber the in-house staff — and a number of them are ex-employees. In these circumstances it is very often hard to find full-time staff members, and when you do you discover they are serving their time before becoming contractors themselves.

Large companies' user departments

User departments will normally afford more autonomy to contractors. Where a contractor is being employed by a user within a large organisation, to circumvent normal employment practice, for instance, the user will tend to rely fairly heavily on him or her. However, the user is unlikely to allow the contractor a high level of authority — to do so would probably invite criticism from the IT department. For instance, large companies who purchase software for personnel management often do so independently of the data processing department. Such systems can be complex to set up and manage — particularly when networks or multi-user computers are involved. Therefore, the personnel department may bring in a data processing contractor, who is given the job of managing all aspects of the technical working of the product. The contractor works directly for the user manager, and is not normally given more than advisory powers.

Mini and microcomputer users

Mini and micro users, on the other hand, who bring in contractors on a facilities management basis, or at a high consultancy level, will often afford them great seniority. In this case, a "consultant" can be merely a senior contractor. Software houses dealing with such customers will often find that they have to deal all the time with the consultant, who has almost total power in the project. Often he or she will actually have accounting or other qualifications, and will be involved in choosing software, as well as project management. "Pure" data processing consultants would not normally be given quite such a high degree of authority as those so qualified. However, the amount of reliance placed by users on such people is often quite extraordinary — and indeed unrealistic.

This sort of relationship has been touched on already. For example, a few years ago, a small software house sold a system to a client. The system did exactly what had been specified, but also came with the ability to be adapted by a user. It was written in interpretive Basic, and therefore easy to modify. The client had a contractor on site, managing things. This contractor decided to make changes to the product, even modifying file structures. The impact of those changes was disastrous. The product needed a number of corrections, to undo the damage. The client, relying on their contractor, would not accept that the fault did not lie with the software supplier, and there was heated argument about who would pay for the corrections.

Nobody came out the winner. The client thought he had bought a poor product. The software supplier knew that the contractor's tampering had done the harm, and the contractor just kept his head down, hoping that the flak would miss him.

Software houses

Software houses make extensive use of contractors. Perhaps realising the value of well-trained people, many software houses rely on their skills for the really clever bits of design, or for their knowledge of new technologies. In-house staff then are trained by, or brought in alongside contractors. In this context, "software houses" can either be firms originating packaged software, or consultancies. The latter firms will often use highly qualified contractors as "associates" — freelance additions to their full-time staff roster. In addition, it is often politically astute of software houses to employ freelancers as sub-contractors to do work contracted by their clients. In this way they can give the appearance of not needing to reject any work because of staff shortages — and also, of course, turn a healthy profit.

This is particularly true of the specialist houses — those concentrating on particular skills or products. If you know a 4GL or DBMS well, it is a good idea to make yourself known to a software house which specialises in that area. To find out who to approach, contact the software supplier and ask them who are their favourite software houses — and who are actively providing staff at the moment. Naturally, since providing this information may not help the software supplier, you should exercise some tact when making such a request. However, quite often you will find that the suppliers are either looking for contract staff themselves, or have sales which will rely on finding such people for their clients — so they will often welcome such an approach.

Sometimes a particular large project will be in the control of one or two software houses. I can think of two Uniface projects in this category. It is then hard for anybody else to get in. The software houses naturally guard these very profitable privileges very carefully — but seldom have enough staff on their books to fulfil them. They then turn to contractors — using general agencies as middle men. With this number of non-productive suppliers between the client and the contractor you can see that this can be a very expensive business for the client company.

Another area in which a software house may use a contractor is to provide specialist services for their clients. For instance, if they need to introduce new technology to a client, for which they do not themselves have sufficient skilled staff, they may employ contractors to fill the gap.

2.3 What skills and skill levels do they require?

Although there is work across almost the whole spectrum of the employment marketplace, one consistent theme is that trainees need not apply. Expected levels of competence tend to be higher in each category than would be expected of an ordinary employee at the same seniority.

In addition, it is extremely unusual for companies to search for generalists. In other words specific skills will be required. This often means that jobs will be specified at the most exact level. For instance, when COBOL programmers were in demand, it would not have taken a lot of effort for a COBOL programmer to learn the differences between one operating system and another, and take on the job. However, many employers are very specific about what machine experience is needed. If you try to tell the agency that you could do a job on, say, IBM, when you have DEC experience, you will probably be told that your skills are not relevant to that.

Nonetheless, where skills are very badly needed, and specialists are scarce, employers have been known to take on people and allow them time to learn the necessary skills. The shortage of C++ skills, for instance, has forced many employers to take on untrained staff, and then train them.

Companies are often far too rigid in specifying skill levels needed. This stems partly from ignorance and partly from a desire to maximise the return on investment in expensive and transient staff. Some IBM mainframe data processing managers do not realise that, for instance, a knowledge of the older database IDMS can very quickly be translated to an understanding of DB2, nor do all DEC managers realise how smoothly a programmer trained on a Unix machine can make the transformation onto a VAX under VMS. However, since many contracts last months or even years, and since most contract staff are at least as diligent as their full-time colleagues, a little time spent in re-training could pay off very handsomely. This area will be covered in more detail in Chapter 7.

As a footnote, for the first edition of this book, one contract agency gave us a list of job requirements currently waiting to be filled. They put a note on the bottom that there were quite a few requirements which had not been mentioned. These had been on their books for some time, and they had no realistic hope of filling them. From such comments, it would appear that there is a buoyant market for "second-hand" skills. Perhaps some enterprising and suitably qualified agency should put some thought into that?

2.4 Teleworking

For many years, it has been fashionable to forecast that home working will become more prevalent. The delivery mechanism would be ever more powerful PCs, the impact of the Internet and the use of dedicated or switched lines to enable a remote worker to hook directly into the client's computers. The most obvious area for such working is computer systems development. After all, nearly all development is done using a PC — either as a terminal to a mini or mainframe, or as the host to the new system. There seems little point in insisting that that PC should reside in an expensive office, and that its user should waste time travelling to and from that office.

This was mentioned in the last book, but is now much more possible. After all, if a system is being developed on PCs, there is little to stop a contractor doing at least some of the work from home. The limitation is mainly imposed by the software environment. It can certainly pay a contractor wishing to work in this way to acquire the necessary hardware and software. I have been lucky enough to be able to do this most of the time for the past ten years. It is very pleasant to sit looking out over the fields whilst working — and going to talk to the horse at the end of the garden when I have a particularly knotty problem to solve.

However, I would stress that working from home — though there are many rational arguments in its favour — is still fairly rare. Whenever contract agencies phone to seduce me with offers of luscious and remunerative jobs in Rhyl or Leeds, I point out that I work from home, where I have a fully equipped office with a network of machines, all the Microsoft software and everything else I need to do their work. The agencies almost universally express amazement at my good fortune, telling me that their clients would not countenance my working for them in that way. Even where they express some encouragement, and agree to discuss the iconoclastic suggestion that I might be able to avoid the daily commute, they never seem to ring back. No, home working is still something that the contract recruitment industry needs to encompass.

The home-working contracts which I have been lucky enough to enjoy have all been directly arranged with my clients. Indeed, though I still talk to agencies, I am pleased to be able to say that I have not needed to have a contract through one of them for some time. My main contract from 1996 to 1998 has been working for a company in Northern Ireland. They were most accommodating to me, and made it easy for me to work from my home most of the time. From their point of view, it means that they got a much longer working day from me — I seldom start later than 8 in the morning, usually finish at around 6 in the evening and often work at weekends. I have all the necessary software in my own name — and have even been in the position of providing them with the only system at the time capable of running the Windows/NT environment used by their clients.

From my point of view the advantages are obvious. I have a very balanced working environment, I can work when I need to (and I do not take advantage of that freedom), and I can operate in a much more flexible way than if I were in the office from nine to five. I have even been able to take work away with me when I have been on holiday — working on a portable computer and connected via a GSM phone to my clients. That is a somewhat double-edged sword — since I never really have an uninterrupted holiday, having always to be on call — but that is a small price to pay for such flexibility. I must express my warm thanks to them for their far-sightedness in this. I would also like to suggest that more companies would benefit from such far-sightedness. If the right controls are in place, there are very few developments which could not be done, at least in part, in such a fashion.

I have tried to persuade agencies to look into teleworking as a solution to their clients' needs. There is no doubt that the teleworking contractor can be particularly effective. However, whenever I suggest it to an agency I am treated as if I have suddenly arrived with a revolutionary new idea from the planet Zog. The agency either dismisses it as dangerously trendy, or, having thought about it (I presume), omits to call me back with any feedback.

I have a suggestion therefore for all those agencies out there trying desperately to find contract staff in the desert of suitable people. Have a go at pushing teleworking. Persuade your clients to give it a go, advertise for some people and see how you get on — you never know, you might start a revolution!

If you are intending to work from home, you will need to discipline yourself in a number of ways. For this section, I am indebted to the proof reader of this edition, who is obviously a fellow teleworker.

The first question I am often asked, when I tell people that I work from home is "don't you find there are too many distractions". The answer is that I do not, or I would not be able to continue. However, I have set things up specifically so that, when I am working, I am not disturbed, nor am I distracted from my work.

I am very lucky to have a separate office, which I can lock up and leave — and which is not used for anything else. In my office I have all the equipment I need, and the necessary software, to enable me to work more productively than were I to visit a client's office. In my office I have a wood-burning stove, which means I can keep warm in winter without needing to heat the whole house, and adequate windows to open in the few warm summer days we have. I have a large work surface and plenty of filing cabinets and bookshelves for all my papers and manuals.

Because I develop software for clients, I make a practice of e-mailing them regular updates — even if only interim versions. That way, if I were to have a disaster, there would be a recent back up off site of the relevant work. I also make sure that I communicate with them frequently — at least twice a week if possible — to keep them up to date with my progress and to enable me to get feedback from them. I also visit my clients regularly. This is important so that we can co-ordinate our work, and control the projects in progress. However, for some work — isolated projects which require no feedback, it is possible not to visit so often. If I have a chunk of documentation to do, for example, which might take some weeks to achieve, I will not visit them during that time — but will keep them updated with the latest versions of documents so that they can check progress if they want — and as back up.

The only disadvantage is that I do not really have days off. I often work over the weekend — and do not necessarily charge for that. I also frequently go into the office when I cannot sleep at night and do something. This means that my clients get more work from me than they would if I had to travel to their offices every day.

Occasionally I have had to go into a client's office to work. This happened recently, at their insistence, because they wanted to be able to see that I was working. The absurd thing was that I found that their own machines were far slower than my own, and I had to offload the relevant portions of the software onto my own machine and use that — otherwise the job would have taken twice as long as I waited for compilations to be done. In fact, in this case, the client needed to communicate with me as I went along because the software being developed was needed very quickly, and was being developed in quite an unstructured fashion.

I would strongly recommend teleworking. I hope that it will really become the norm in the future. The benefits in terms of productivity are very noticeable. It is not everybody's cup of tea, but if you can work on your own, you can have a much more comfortable life — and get through much more work.

3 | What it takes to become a contract worker

3.1 Introduction

The opening chapters have described why companies use contract workers, and what sort of job they are expected to do. As has already been said, this sort of work is not everybody's cup of tea. If you are looking for job security, routine and authority, then contracting is unlikely to appeal to you.

Contracting offers significant opportunities for DP staff to sell their skills. Conventional company structures have tended to put restrictions on recruitment of suitably qualified staff. For instance, in the Civil Service, programming staff, on seniority alone may only be at Executive Officer level. However, the Civil Service pay structure limits the payment of such staff. Therefore, to attract experienced data processing staff, the Civil Service often finds it necessary to regrade them as Higher Executive Officers, to attract suitable people from outside. Even then, because of the general employment market, it has been hard for organisations to retain staff without constant regrading.

Outside the Civil Service, computer staff have for many years been able to command high salaries, beyond those enjoyed by personnel with a similar level of seniority or experience. This has, in its turn, enabled skilled staff to improve their earnings significantly by becoming self-employed. This enables companies to bypass normal restrictions on pay, and to find specifically qualified staff on a long or short-term basis. For the contractor, the result is usually a significant increase in earnings. However, although there might appear to be a compelling argument for all with suitable expertise to become self-employed, there are definite disadvantages, and the life will not suit everyone. Success is not guaranteed. It is actually possible to earn less as a contractor than as a full-time employee, and to have far less flexibility in your life.

Contractors working today are in the main as professional as they have ever been. There may be some who have a loose grasp of the truth, and who are happy to sell their dubious skills to one company after another, and then to move on when they are found out, pocketing a fair sum of money on the way. On the other hand there are far more people around with not only good experience, but also a deep background. This background can come from formal education — there are many computer science graduates on the market — or by self-teaching, now that computers are in the reach of most people's purses.

In many ways, a contract, particularly long-term, feels like full-time employment. However there is no doubt that contractors are different from the majority of data processing professionals. In this chapter we will investigate those differences, and explain why this must be so.

3.2 Motivations behind becoming a contractor

The most obvious motivation is financial. For an experienced DP person, with no aspirations to management, but a desire to earn good money, contracting is very attractive. As will be shown in a later chapter, you can generally earn more on contract than you would in full-time employment.

However, the old cliché does apply — money is not everything — though, whoever said that money does not buy you happiness was probably shopping in the wrong store. There are short-term inconveniences, such as the use of contractors to do mundane jobs, and that contracting can involve travel to, and living in, inhospitable places. Though these are often more than compensated for by the extra cash, many contractors turn back to full-time employment. This often happens when they marry or have children. Being a contractor can require a free spirit.

There are other reasons. The computer industry is one which attracts all sorts of folk. Many have learnt to program at home or school, and drifted into the industry. Their hearts are not fully committed to it. For instance, some years ago, a South African was working in London as a contract programmer. He had bought himself a new XJ6 to take home with him. His real ambition was to be a television producer. So, when South African television broadcasts began, he and his car went back home. In the meantime, he had managed to earn very good money, as well as exposing himself to the techniques of TV in this country.

My own case is not dissimilar. As I have said in Chapter 1, I am a writer and a professional singer. Unfortunately neither job yields enough to pay my bills. However, I have been fortunate enough to find computer contracts which I can do from home, in my own time. These enable me to continue to pursue my other careers. I have a splendid little Dell portable computer on which I keep my current work. So I go to a rehearsal, set the machine compiling and then go and kill Carmen. The wonderful thing about it is that I enjoy all three jobs — and I'm never bored.

Boring jobs probably abound in contracting — more so than in full-time employment — but these are so much less significant because of the short-term nature of the work. After all, you are your own boss, and can, within reason, up sticks and go and look for more interesting work fairly easily — without damaging your career.

There are some "career" contractors — people who have no desire to fit into a company hierarchy or attain seniority or who have a yen for travel and variety which cannot easily be fulfilled within a full-time job. Whatever the reason, contractors need to have a different combination of attributes for success than those normally found in DP staff.

In an edition of *Computer Weekly* in 1989, a survey was published which looked at the reasons why people became contractors. It confirmed the reasons already stated — and it also reinforced the view that contractors are not merely out for huge amounts of extra loot.

The reasons given for changing jobs interesting, and are summarised in Table 3.1 — for both contractors and those in a permanent job:

Table 3.1: Reasons for contracting

Reason	Permanent	Contract
Broadening experience	37	31
Increasing salary	31	32
Increasing responsibility	25	7
Family reasons	12	11
Redundancy	10	—
Others	17	19

Although this tends to confirm the opinion that contractors are more money minded that others — the difference is not huge. However, it does highlight the contractor's lack of need for responsibility. Actually, this is not as simple as it seems. In another survey, contractors were found to be far less interested in internal politics than other staff — particularly senior staff, who seem to relish it. Since increased responsibility nearly always brings increased politics, it is not surprising that those who become contractors need neither as much as others. Perhaps DP managers should bear that in mind, and make life less political for permanent technical staff, if they want to retain them.

Continuing this theme, the *Computer Weekly* survey looked at the most important factors in choosing a contract (see Table 2) — the units are number of people in the overall survey.

The figures for contractors are really not far away from those for permanent employees. However, contractors are less worried about being praised for their achievements, and are much more interested in broadening their base of knowledge. Indeed, permanent staff

Table 2:
Factors in
choosing a
contract

Reason	Permanent	Contract
Salary	69	74
Sufficiently demanding problems	81	72
Demands on quality	70	69
Using the best range of expertise	72	67
Feedback on achievement level	76	67
Being consulted by management on changes	74	60
Broadening of experience on OS etc.	59	—
Clear guidelines	62	58
Broadening of experience on applications	53	—
Documentation of system on which you work	51	—

were also far less satisfied with the opportunities offered to broaden their knowledge — a perennial problem. Another fact which came up was that the average length of a contract was far longer than expected, at between six to eighteen months. By contrast, permanent employees spend, on average, only three and a half years in a job — and 27 per cent move within a year. In other words, there is not a heap of difference in job length between contractors and permanent staff. Contractors also were far less willing to contemplate moving house for a new job.

Although contractors have a reputation for being loners, there was no significant difference in their working preferences. 46 per cent preferred working in groups of two to four, and 31 per cent in groups of five to seven. Only 10 per cent preferred to work alone.

Contractors were more satisfied than permanent staff with salaries (66 per cent as opposed to 54 per cent) — salaries averaged £45,000 as opposed to £22,000 for permanent staff. Perhaps this explains why they do not express a feeling of being salary-driven.

Another factor which has driven people into contracting is redundancy. There have been quite a few stories in recent years of people made redundant during the bad old days of the late 1980s who moved into contracting as a short-term expedient before returning to "proper" work. Often they would have approached agencies looking for senior positions and turned down because they were too old and were redundant — which tended to make them less attractive. In desperation they turned to contracting, to find that there were jobs-a-plenty, with more money than they had earned before, and excellent prospects of that income continuing. For many middle to senior managers, experienced in negotiating and management of their personal affairs, these jobs were just the ticket they needed to get back some pride in themselves. Often the stories end with a statement that they would not dream of going back into full-time employment — they are far too happy running their small business and controlling their own lives.

3.3 Experience

It has been established that trainees need not apply to become contract workers. Companies will typically be paying around twice the normal employee rate to employ them. For that fee, they will not expect to have to provide time and money to train people — except in the most rudimentary way. Of course, if an employer has accepted that a particular contractor has related skills, and is happy to allow time to translate those into the requirement, time will be allotted. For instance, an SCO Unix C programmer employed by an HP user would be given time to learn the different operating system. However, the contractor in this case will have had to convince his employer that he has the relevant ability and experience.

There is an increasing pool of PC users who have taught themselves or done courses. They have little data processing experience, in conventional terms, but they bring to the business a lot of practical knowledge from playing around at home and college. They now represent one of the few groups of relatively inexperienced staff who can, as long as they can find contracts, make a living contracting. Knowledge of such packages as Word, dBase or Lotus make such people saleable. However, though there are contracts around for such experience, it is a very transient marketplace. The differences, for instance, between Word for Windows version 2 and version 6 are not insignificant. If you know the former you can use the latter, but you will not be an expert. The field is changing very rapidly, and it would be advisable for such people to ensure that they broaden their knowledge and experience as quickly as they can, to widen their marketability.

The way in which such experience is gained is normally in the field, in full-time employment. However good his or her sparkling new degree may look and feel, it is unlikely that a new graduate will be instantly taken on as a contract worker in the commercial field. Skills must be relevant — and few degree courses cover commercial data processing in sufficient detail. Not all contracts involve commercial work, however. A well-qualified graduate or postgraduate may well find he or she can move directly into a scientific contract.

Although experience is essential, there are times when you can transfer into new areas without direct knowledge of a particular field or technique. These are either fortuitous or calculated.

It often happens that, once you have been accepted in a contracting situation, you are asked to look at another area — one in which you have no direct experience, but one that you can learn. For instance, when working as an analyst you may become interested in, and teach yourself, a new skill like a particular programming language, or analytical technique in the idle time which any job involves. When that skill becomes needed either by the current employer, or by another company, you should be able to sell it. This is the fortuitous way of gaining knowledge.

The calculated way may be rather more costly. A contractor with good general expertise may be able to increase his or her bargaining ability by paying to go on a course and learn a new skill. For instance an experienced mainframe programmer/analyst, who has worked mainly on large systems, could easily go on a Visual Basic course at his or her own expense. This would open a new range of possibilities for freelance work. It is also likely to impress a potential employer, who will normally admire the contractor's enterprise.

Experience is necessary. Indeed, there is a crying need for industry specific experience over and above mere data processing knowledge. However it is not enough by itself. Contractors need a number of other skills, less usual in the normal jobs market.

3.4 Need for flexibility

The contractor must be flexible. However much a particular speciality may appeal to you, you must be prepared to ditch it if a particular contract comes along which does not require it. For instance, you may be particularly interested in accounting systems design. However, many companies are buying packages for such systems, and there may not be suitable jobs available for you at a particular time. It would be unwise to wait for such a contract to come up, and to turn down another sufficiently lucrative job for which you are qualified. If you really want to specialise, you would probably be better taking a full-time job.

In addition, it is desirable for you as a contractor to be prepared to take the more mundane and boring jobs. This is unfortunate, but not surprising. After all the employer may well have employed you only because the work is not popular in-house.

Flexibility is necessary in other ways, too. You may absolutely hate the sight of Windows, and think that it has been designed by a committee of chimpanzees taking time off from trying to recreate the works of Shakespeare. You may think that the whole object-oriented debate is a complete load of hogwash. However, you cannot escape from the fact that these two things are the most sought-after in the whole business. So go out and learn Windows; be object-oriented and go with the flow. If you do not, you might as well take up farming.

3.5 Interview techniques

Any prospective full-time employee looking for a new job needs to be presentable at interview. However, particularly where the job sought is "boffin like", employers may make allowances for rough manner or lack of presentability. This reflects the state of the job market as much as anything else.

However, contractors are in a rather different category. For many reasons, the contractor must be able, chameleon like, to blend with different surroundings. The employer often only has one meeting, the interview, in which he can assess your potential. Because you will change jobs far more frequently than a full-time employee, you must hone your interview skills. You need to be a good, gentle salesman, sensitive to your target, and able to demonstrate how well you can fit his needs.

This means that not only must you look presentable, and be able to show your skills, but also you must be capable of weighing up your prospective employer, and deciding how heavily you present yourself. You may well actually have more experience than him. However it is unwise to make this obvious, unless he is looking for that degree of skill. Intellectual arrogance can be a hindrance.

Incidentally, because contract work involves by definition a non-employed status, you have no recourse to employment law if you feel aggrieved about your interview. This applies, for instance, to members of ethnic minorities and women. People can appeal to ACAS (Advisory, Conciliation and Arbitration Service, see Chapter 2) if they feel that they have been rejected for work purely on the grounds of race or sex. If their appeal is upheld, the prospective employer can be made to take them on, or pay them compensation. This would not be possible for contractors.

3.6 Self-sufficiency

You will, however long you work with the same employer, never belong to that company. You are unlikely to be treated badly, but there will be parts of the company's activities to which you will not be welcomed. For instance, many companies hold staff meetings to discuss such mundane items as the company attitude to smoking, or the quality of the coffee. It is likely that these will not be open to contractors. Of course, you have to be careful that you do not appear to align yourself with other contractors on those occasions — becoming a separate little clique of your own!

If you have a deep need of a feeling of belonging, then contracting will not be suitable for you — however well you fit in with the rest of the criteria. It can be very lonely to be left in an empty office, while everybody else is called in to a "pep up" meeting.

The same feeling will apply to your relationships with your peers within the company. Many full-time staff resent contractors. After all, they know that freelancers are being paid significantly higher rates, and often feel that they are no more competent. A contractor must be both thick-skinned and sensitive to handle such feelings. After all, if you cannot get on with other staff members, you are unlikely to last long in the contract.

One last aspect of being a "loner" is being forced to stay away from home. London contracts are normally within reasonable commuting distance for a Greater London resident, and there are enough to choose from to ensure that you will not need to stay away from home. However, the rest of the country is not so lucky. Contractors from Leeds, for instance, may find that their only option is to stay in a hotel for weeks on end, coming home only at weekends. Such is often the contractor's lot.

Many employees do not realise just how much their company actually does for them. Your taxes are all dealt with, your National Insurance contributions records are kept up-to-date, you will receive payment when you are ill, or if you have a family catastrophe. Your holidays are paid for and you can usually go away confident in the knowledge that your job will be waiting for you when you return. Your company will probably run a pension scheme, which will all be dealt with for you by them.

Become a contractor, and these, and many other aspects of your life, will become your sole responsibility. Your ability to handle your own life without help from your employer will probably be the most significant factor determining your success as a contractor. If you are not able to do this, you would be far better off remaining a full-time employee. Indeed, this is one of the fundamental reasons why contractors need to be paid more than full-time staff.

3.7 Sick pay

If you are ill, you will not be paid. Therefore it is prudent to have some kind of insurance to cover this. Even visits to doctor or dentist will not be paid — unless you have a very understanding and flexible employer.

Many office workers have private health care schemes provided by their employers. These often apply to their families as well. It is not altruism on the part of employers to provide this care — the sooner a sick employee is healthy again, the sooner he or she will become productive. Family ill-health can also cut deeply into a worker's concentration.

The same applies to you as a contractor. However, the biggest loser here is you yourself. If you are sick, your earnings will stop. If you are unproductive, your contract may be terminated. Even in a sellers' market, you cannot work if you are unwell. You must make sure you can survive on your own resources in case you get ill. I have already mentioned the question of cover during periods of sickness (see Chapter 1).

3.8 Holiday pay

You can take more holiday than normal as a contractor — between contracts. However, because you will have no holiday pay, you must budget for this time off. It is very sensible to have a plan for holidays. Many contractors have a separate account, into which they put money to pay their expenses while on holiday. Unless there are sufficient funds, they do not take holidays.

It is also important to ensure that you have work to return to after being away. It may be more sensible to negotiate a "hole" in a current contract, rather than flying off into the blue yonder at the end in the fervent hope that something will turn up when you return. The clever contractors manage to work through the winter and then take four months in the sun in the summer. That actually takes an awful lot of careful planning.

In practice it is quite common for contractors not to have much time for holidays. Because they want to be able to accept contracts "back to back", they often cannot be away between. Moreover, they must constantly be looking for the next contract whilst they are working on the current one. That means that they cannot go away until the next contract is settled. But contracts are nearly always set up late in the day, and for nearly immediate start. Therefore the contractor — particularly one working on relatively short contracts — will often not be able to get away at all.

All work and no play makes Jack a dull boy. You should take advantage of your status to enjoy periods of inactivity. It is a real luxury to be able to take a long holiday in the knowledge that you are not impacting your company's schedules, and knowing that you can work hard to make enough money to pay for the break.

3.9 Contracting versus full-time employment

There are many fringe benefits available to full-time employees. Some, such as company cars, are obvious. Others, such as pension schemes, holiday pay and National Insurance payments, are less so. On the other hand the contractor too has many fringe benefits of a different type.

Promotion prospects

It has already been said that there are few promotion prospects, status or management opportunities for contractors. These may not be seen as obvious fringe benefits, but they do exist. If status is important to you, it may be sensible to remain employed.

However, you have status as an expert, which grows with experience. You will achieve your own form of promotion as you move through the levels — from programmer to senior programmer or analyst, to specialist. You may not have people reporting to you — though that can happen to contract project leaders — but you will have your own career progression.

Job security

Job security is a benefit not afforded in the same measure to the contractor. However, these day this only really applies after two years of employment. In some ways, a long-term contract can actually offer more job security in its early period. However, a contractor only has recourse to civil law in the event of a dispute, and this is far more expensive, time-consuming and hazard-prone than is an employment tribunal.

These days, jobs are far less secure than they have ever been. Much has been written recently about the way in which particularly middle managers are losing their jobs, and forced, with inadequate pension provisions and a fiercely competitive job market, to take what they would consider a very lowly job, like driving a mini-cab.

For a contractor, such security is not there, and never has been. His security comes from having, maintaining and developing well grounded and marketable skills — unlike, perhaps, those unfortunate middle managers.

Miscellaneous services

Most companies offer backup services to employees. For instance, discount rates for car purchase and insurance are available from some companies. Company-subsidised meals are often available — contractors are usually able to participate if meals are provided in-house, but they will not be given luncheon vouchers.

One reason why some people become contractors is to increase the flexibility of their working. They imagine that, because they are paid only when they work, they can take time off, within reason, when they need it. In practice this is very seldom the case. Contractors are usually brought in because there is a shortage of staff, or a time constraint on a project. Therefore, there is work to be done, and a time limit in which to do it. In addition, it can cause, albeit unjustified, resentment among full-time staff if contractors are seen swanning around having lots of days off. Many companies will not allow any break from normal 9-5 work even when there is no actual work to be done within that time. This may be an attempt to keep the rest of the staff motivated, ensuring that, should any work turn up, it can be done promptly — or it may be sheer bloody-mindedness.

Contractors often choose to be self-employed because they have other irons in the fire. It is something of a shock, therefore, to find that a client still expects a full, normal week. One contractor, who needed to have some time off for his other pursuits was shocked to be told that, although he was completing his work ahead of time, and spent much of his time waiting for resources, he could have no days off, despite the fact that these would be unpaid. He had to part company with the client over this. Maybe this should not have been such a surprise — but it seemed illogical to pay somebody unnecessarily to do nothing. In practice, you should expect to work like a normal employee (and often considerably harder), and not be shown any special considerations unless you specifically agree these with the client.

Another factor which often arises in contracting is overtime. You are contracted, normally, to do a number of hours per week, 35 or 37.5 being the most normal. It is usual that any hours worked over and above that number will be paid for, normally at a higher rate. Such overtime has to agreed with the supervisor, but the nature of the work, and its urgency, usually dictate that there is little dissension in practice.

Contract work should bring variety. You can, to some extent, choose the length of the contract when you are deciding which to apply for. Contracts are advertised with a length, expressed in months or weeks. However, it is very normal for contracts to run beyond this time. In extreme cases, contracts have extended for years beyond their original length. This is not guaranteed, however, and until an extension is specifically agreed, it is wise to assume that a contract will only run its length. Although work may be varied it is often very dull. As has already been established, contractors are often given the work full-time staff have rejected. Therefore conversions, maintenance and report programming are more normal than software design, or exciting programming projects.

Contracting carries no employment rights — depending on terms a contract may be cut at short notice for almost any reason. That is not to say that contracting cannot offer security, particularly if a long-term is built into the contract. However, by the same token, you are not able then to go and find a more stimulating project if you want to until the term has expired. You have, as has been stated, no employment protection, and civil courts are not so amenable as Industrial Tribunals.

Earnings are generally good. If they were not, there would be little point in contracting. However, contracting needs very careful management, to ensure that enough provision is made for tax, time off, etc. This will be covered in Chapter 6.

It is not unusual for contractors to become so much a part of the company that they are asked to become full-time staff members. It is quite an accolade, and gives you a sense of real achievement if you are judged to be good enough to be asked to join the company. However, it can be a dangerous move, unless you are really certain. The first reason for this is that your relationship as a contractor is slightly different from an employee's. Because you are an outsider, you can be more objective, and perhaps more critical. You are likely to have a more equal relationship with your manager — because you are probably considered to be an expert. As soon as you join the company, you must change these attitudes — and that can be tricky.

Another problem which can arise is with the agency, if you were introduced by one. They will expect to be paid an introduction fee, usually of the order of 15 per cent of salary. This can be a problem, since employers may be loathe to pay. They have been known to ask contractors to pretend not to be there any more, so that the employer can bypass the fee. Naturally the advice here is not to be led into accepting such an arrangement — you will probably be the one to suffer.

Contracting work is different from full-time employment. You are paid more to do a generally less interesting job. You have to manage your affairs more carefully, and less is done for you. You do not belong to a comfortable group. You are unlikely to be involved deeply in the affairs of that company. Lastly, you have a different relationship with your manager than a full-time employee.

4 Forming your own company

4.1 Introduction

Before starting this chapter, I would stress the very sensible advice given by almost all contract agencies. When dealing with all matters legal and financial it is wise indeed to consult a professional adviser. For the purpose of contracting, where you will primarily need tax advice, the obvious person with whom to deal is an accountant.

Becoming self-employed is not actually as simple a matter as it might at first appear. You cannot simply elect to be self-employed if you continue to draw the majority — or the whole — of your income from one source. Even were you to say "I am now self-employed", your employer would have a duty to continue to deduct tax and National Insurance contributions from your salary. The old days when contract workers could elect to be taxed on "Schedule D" are past. This is the basis on which actors, for instance, are employed. They are thereby entitled to declare their income yearly, and may claim many expenses against tax. Actors' Equity — the performers' union — has been fighting hard to retain this status even for its members. You can only justify a claim to be genuinely self-employed if you have multiple — and equally lucrative — sources of income. Even then, your accountant may have to argue hard and long with the Inland Revenue to justify your claim.

The reasons for this attitude on the part of the authorities is that, in the past, many full-time employees were becoming self-employed merely as a tax evasion exercise. Nor is this unique to the United Kingdom. In America there has been an enormous fuss over changes in taxation legislation which have removed even the protection of the limited liability corporation, where this is seen as being created solely for the purpose of tax evasion. The same might happen in this country – contractors and agencies are often lobbying to prevent such changes in status.

As a contractor, whether contracted directly to a company or via an agency, somebody has a duty to ensure that tax is paid on your earnings. Normal contract staff will be given two choices. Either you are paid by the agency or company on a net basis (they will deduct and manage your PAYE and National Insurance), or you must form or join a company which will then have the duty of accounting for tax. That company will almost invariably be required to register for VAT – so that VAT may be levied on your invoices and be claimed against the contractee's VAT liability. The reason for this insistence seems to be that it confers legitimacy on the arrangement – if you are VAT registered, you seem to be a substantial operation, rather than an individual trying to avoid your responsibilities to the State. In addition, it is unlikely that you will be earning far below the earnings threshold, and the agencies will want to be seen to encourage you to obey the law.

4.2 Two methods of being self-employed

For the contractor there are, in theory at least, two possible methods of being self-employed. In practice, few contractors use these – the majority establish limited companies.

Self-employment (sole trader)

The first is self-employment, which has already been dealt with. Self-employed people are very unusual in computer contracting, but are prevalent in shop-keeping, antique dealing, plumbing etc. These are trades where you are very much responsible for your own management, rather than reporting to somebody else. The self-employed person does not have the benefit of limited liability (see below).

The sort of people who nowadays can claim to be genuinely self-employed are those who, on a continuing basis, can show that they are serving a number of different employers, equally, at the same time. For instance, many freelance musicians go from gig to gig, never being employed by the same person for any length of time. In addition, much of the work overlaps, so on any one day they may be employed by more than one company. This is obviously radically different from the situation of the typical contractor, who will draw income from the same company for a considerable time.

The only category of contractor who may be able to claim genuine self-employment is the true consultant, who works on multiple short contracts, often simultaneously. The problem, from an agency's viewpoint, is that it is their duty as your contractee to ensure that tax is paid. Therefore few, if any, agencies will accept that you are self-employed.

Another term for the same thing is the sole trader. This means that you are a single individual, rather than two or more (see below). You may be trading under your own, or another name, and you may register for VAT.

Until 1995, self-employed people produced a tax return based on income in the previous tax year, on which tax will be payable a year ahead. Thus you would have paid tax for 1995 in 1997. However, this system has changed, and the Inland Revenue has slid the year back, so that you will now pay tax only one year in arrears. If you are self-employed, it is wise to ask an accountant to calculate the impact of this change. You may benefit by taking this opportunity to alter your "year end" — but your accountant can advise you.

Partnerships

The second form is as a partner. This is a status which, particularly in the higher echelons of consultancy, has a far more solid feel. A partnership (or "firm") consists of two or more individuals. It has no separate legal identity — except in Scottish partnerships — and its members are individually liable for its debts. Although it is normal to write a partnership agreement, the Partnership Act of 1890 merely defines a partnerships as "the relation which subsists between persons carrying on a business in common with a view to profit". The maximum allowable number of partners (with some exceptions not relevant here) is twenty.

Partnerships are very much relationships of trust, since each partner must accept the responsibility for the actions of all others – they are defined as being each others' agencies. Although in general partners are equally liable for the debts of the partnership, a limited partnership can be written, as long as one member accepts overall responsibility for the debts. This is highly unusual. The normal way to limit liability is to form a limited company (see below).

Partnerships are usual for professionals, such as lawyers and accountants. This is established by both practice and professional ethics, particularly for the former group. A partnership can be said to display a high moral standpoint, since its members take full responsibility for its affairs. This is not just claptrap. A lawyer practising in a limited liability company rather than a partnership, for instance, could simply walk way from a badly bodged case, leaving his clients out of pocket, and only able to be compensated from the already spoken for assets of a bankrupt company. He could then start the next day with a new company, and continue to trade until a further disaster befell another hapless client. In a partnership that would be impossible. Partnerships do not protect the individual from bad work. However they do demonstrate that the members accept their duties. For this reason, the Law Society has rules which prevent conventional legal practices from limiting their liability.

Partnerships are often felt to be attractive by would-be professionals. For example, management consultants frequently form themselves into partnerships. This is as much for marketing as anything else. The impression given of ethicality and high moral tone no doubt helps. Partnerships certainly are relevant for higher levels of contracting. If you are working with a number of other like-minded individuals, a partnership might be attractive. It is cheaper to establish than a limited company. However you may still have problems convincing agencies and the tax man of your legitimacy. Also, if any individual partner gets into financial difficulties, it can affect all the others. The most common financial disaster to befall a solicitor is probably when his or her unscrupulous partner disappears with the funds, leaving the hapless individual to pay all the debts. I have met more than one solicitor in this state.

Contracts made with a partnership are enforceable on the members of that partnership personally. This is in marked contrast with the limited company. What it means is that, should any partner undertake a debt on behalf of the partnership, that becomes the debt of all. Worse still, the debt is unlimited. In other words, if your crooked partner borrowed £100,000 from a bank and then did a runner to the Cayman Islands, you'd probably lose your house. Your only recourse would be a legal case against the dishonest partner. Given the fact that he was now sunning himself far from home, such recourse would be about as useful as a non-smoking cigarette.

4.3 Limited liability companies

A limited company is actually a separate legal entity. The liability for its debts is limited, usually to the nominal value of its issued shares. This is, in practice, for the small business, £100. The shareholders themselves cannot be sued directly for the debts of the company.

A contract made with a limited company can only be enforced with that company, not with its members. In addition, directors of limited companies can have contracts of employment with those companies. Thus you can become a member of a company which then has the contract with the contractee. Your company is paid for your services, and pays you a salary, net of tax. The company has a responsibility to manage the PAYE. However, the company itself may spend part of that money, before tax, on legitimate expenses. For instance you may be able to acquire a car, or a personal computer — both entirely reasonable business items. These can be paid for by the company in as tax-efficient way as possible. See Chapter 6 for more details.

Although two or more people used to be needed to form a limited liability company, it is now possible to have single shareholder companies. It is only necessary to stipulate that the company has a single shareholder. Normally you will have a second shareholder, who can be a purely nominal appointee, your spouse or a friend, for example. This second person will, however, be a company functionary (and often the legal company secretary), and entitled to make decisions on behalf of the company. Therefore, even though your liabilities are limited, mischief could be caused by an unscrupulous director. Make sure that you know, trust and can, if necessary, control your other director. Making the second person company secretary can help, since it can make him or her responsible for any legal problems which might arise. However, this is a purely notional advantage — company secretaries may be legally liable, but, if they cannot be reached, the weight will fall on you.

Limited liability companies, as their name suggests, operate under the protection of law. If the company finds itself in debt, and is unable to pay, it can be liquidated, with debts still outstanding. These debts will then become the responsibility of the liquidator, or receiver, who will pay whatever proportion is possible out of the company's assets. However, there are two major areas in which the concept of limited liability does not apply. If, when a company fails, it owes tax or National Insurance payments, its directors can be personally liable for these debts. However, the Inland Revenue takes a pragmatic attitude in these matters, and, if you genuinely cannot pay these debts, they will be unlikely to pursue you.

As a contractor, you will certainly be encouraged by agencies to form and operate a limited company. From the legal and fiscal viewpoint it is the soundest path. It costs a certain amount, but is often worth the expense.

There are two aspects to running a limited company which should, however, be stressed. Firstly, you will need a bank account. Banks charge small businesses on every transaction. They also charge a "management fee", and they do not pay interest on current business accounts. Their charges are often waived in the first year, but after that, remember that you will have to allow for quarterly charges of around £30. This may not seem much — but it is irksome, compared to the charge-free and interest-bearing personal accounts to which we are accustomed.

Secondly, you will almost invariably be made to sign a personal guarantee for any borrowings, such as car leases or bank overdrafts. A friend of mine runs a very successful hi-fi business. He built it from nothing to the point where it is now turning over more than £4 million per annum. Along the way he was made to sign a personal guarantee, and the bank insisted subsequently on linking this to his house. Once his business became cash rich, he asked the bank to return the guarantee. Their immediate reaction was to retain the deeds to the house "in case we need them later". The whole business was sorted out very amicably in the end, and he now has the returned guarantee framed. However, banks are not at all the helpful people they would like to have us believe. As a small business, you will run into new ways of being parted from your money that you would not have even contemplated.

4.4 How to acquire your company

Buying a company will cost you between £180 and £450. There are a number of ways to set up a company. Easiest by far is the "off the shelf" company formation specialist. Their job is to set up companies, usually with names which bear no relation to the actual owners of the company. The names in fact often have been assembled by connecting two or more unrelated words together. For example "Floorland" was the name of a shelf company. They will find a suitable company from their portfolio, and arrange the paperwork to transfer its ownership to you. In addition its name can be changed by them to something more relevant. This will incur a small cost — around £40.

Companies have papers, known as the Memorandum and Articles of Association (known in the trade as "Memo and Arts"). These contain a number of legal necessities, one of which is the "General Objects" clause, in which they make a statement defining what business they actually intend to follow. A General Objects clause will probably have a general catchall phrase enabling the company to carry out:

"other business which the directors may deem fit from time to time".

Apart from the Objects clause, "Memo and Arts" are fairly standard. Your accountant can brief you as necessary.

It is advisable to buy a new company, rather than picking one up which has been trading previously. It is amazing how problems which are not of your making can suddenly surface and cause no end of trouble. Since Companies house has Crown Immunity, if it has made mistakes in the earlier administration of the company, you can end up with expensive problems.

For example, a company was set up some years ago by directors from another company. At that time the new company was not actually used — it was intended for a purpose which never saw fruition. The other company was taken over, and its founders left. They started to trade using the new company. They registered for VAT, opened bank accounts, and raised invoices, which were paid. Suddenly — two and a half years after they had left the original company — they received notification that their bank account was frozen, because the new owners of the original company had told Companies House that the new company was not needed. The new owners had not been entitled to act in that way. However, Companies House should never have accepted the changes. They had come from people who clearly were not officers of the company. Nevertheless, the money remained tied up in the bank account, and the whole mess is still not cleared up. It is certain that the one group who will not make amends in any way is Companies House — even though they are the ones who quite incorrectly accepted the word of people who were clearly not entitled to act. Had the founders of the company used a new, unsullied, company, they would not have had those difficulties.

As an alternative to the off-the-shelf company, you can have a custom-built company formed for you, with your own Memo and Arts. This will cost more (of the order of £450, rather than around £180). There seems little purpose in this, for contracting, unless you want to make the company able to do something specific — like developing products to sell abroad.

In practice, you can rely on your accountant to do all the work of setting up the company. This will involve creating the company's books, possibly acquiring a company seal (used for all official papers, and normally retained by the accountant — though this is no longer a legal necessity), issuing shares and all the paperwork involved. The only job you will need to do will be to open a bank account — and your bank manager will advise you on that.

4.5 Who's who within the company

Shareholders

A company consists of two groups, who often are the same people. The members of a company are called the shareholders. They are the people who actually put up the money to start the company, and who are entitled to a share in its profits. With the sort of tiny company formed for contractors, the shareholders may only pay for two shares of the one hundred which make up the total share capital. Many accountants will set up larger quantities of authorised shares — though it makes little difference to the contractor. The only time when you might need to pay for all the shares is if you are raising substantial sums — perhaps to allow you to develop a product or extend the business. It will not affect your position in regard to normal operations, including being given an overdraft facility.

Shares can be confusing. As the owner of the company, you will be asked to pay some money for its shares. The normal – or "authorised" "share capital" of a private limited company is £100. This means that the liabilities of the company are limited to that amount. £100 worth of shares will be available – but it is unusual for them to be issued ("paid up") in full. You will normally only pay for a single £1 share per founding shareholder initially. The other "unissued" shares would only become payable if the company was sold. Shares mark the ownership of the company. It is quite normal to leave a large portion of the company's authorised share capital unissued, for later use. For instance, if your company expands and you want to bring in other members, you may decide to issue some more shares to them and to the founders, to realign the proportions owned to reflect the work done by the original shareholders. This can be done easily if you have unissued shares.

Owning shares in a private limited company is not like owning shares in a public company. In the latter case you can trade them on the Stock Exchange, or other markets. Your shares for your company will have no value to anyone other than yourself unless you are successful beyond your expectations as a contractor, and bring the company to market, or you sell the company on for someone else's use.

Directors

The other group are the directors, the "officers" of the company. The directors have the job of actually running the company, although they need not actually be employed by it. The powers and duties are defined in the company's Articles of Association. They have a duty to hold board meetings, and minutes must be recorded of such meetings. The size of the quorum (the minimum number which constitutes a legal meeting) is defined in the Articles – the normal size is two. The first papers which you, as a director of a new company will see, apart from the Memo and Arts, are the form which registers you as a director, and probably a board minute to open a bank account in the company's name. This latter document, printed by the banks, typifies the difference between working as an individual, and a company. You will sign many such minutes which describe meetings — it all sounds grand, but in practice they are just legal pieces of paper. That is not to say that they are not important legal instruments which must correctly represent your running of the business. You must act with integrity at all times — and understand the import of all your actions.

You are entitled to have a company with only one director, but it is more normal to have a minimum of two. In addition, the company will also need a company secretary. This can be one of the directors, unless there is only one. The company secretary is responsible for convening meetings, and for arranging that the relevant paperwork with relation to the company is done. It is normally advisable, unless you have experience of such matters, to let your accountant act as company secretary. However, an accountant may not act as both auditor and company secretary. Most accountants get around this by offering a company secretarial service, whereby they, or a closely allied firm, do the work on behalf of the actual company secretary.

One matter which is changing is that companies turning over below £250,000 no longer have to have a full audit each year. They need only prepare their accounts in accordance with the layout which would be produced during an audit. This should slightly reduce the costs on small limited companies — though the preparation of figures will still be necessary. In fact, the general view is that this change has made very little difference, and auditors are still preparing very similar accounts to those prepared in former years.

4.6 Miscellaneous matters

Your company must have a registered office. This is the address to which all formal communication will be sent. Normally this will be the address of your accountant. Most accountants' offices have lists of companies whose registered office they provide. Companies House only write to the company's registered office.

As a company, you will need to account for all income and expenditure, and this will need to be subjected to periodic audit by an impartial accounting firm. This is a statutory requirement – not at all unreasonable. See Chapter 6 for more details.

4.7 Consortia of contractors

One idea which has been successfully practised by some contractors is that of forming a consortium. This can be used in a variety of ways, but chiefly can spread both administrative workload and cost.

The company is an ideal vehicle for such a consortium. A group of contractors can pool their resources, set up a company as shareholders, and then be subject only to one set of audit and accounting fees. As long as there is both trust and agreement on the division of the income, individuals' shares can be significantly improved in this way.

One group of contractors reportedly even go so far as to pool the income, and divide it out between them. If a member goes through a bad patch, without a contract, he or she can be supported by the others. Quite how far such an apparently civilised idea can be taken depends on the individuals. Obviously a lazy partner could easily live off the earnings of his more diligent partners.

In the particular case, the members all drew salaries. All could, to a limit prescribed, use company money to buy cars or other items. Naturally, as a group they had more substance than an individual, and could negotiate accordingly. Such a scheme is unusual, but it could be a very attractive way for contractors both to reduce costs and to insure themselves against possible idle time. Actually to have made it work is quite a feat.

In practice, these consortia can prove far more expensive to the individual than a simple company, and are best avoided.

5 How to find your first contract

5.1 Introduction

Once you have decided to become a contractor, you can't simply resign your job and wait for the contract to arrive. You must hunt for a suitable job. Finding a contract is exactly like any other job search. There are many agencies around, most of which deal with both contract and permanent staff. They advertise mainly in the weekly computer press. You apply to them for contracts, they interview you, the client interviews you and Bob's your uncle. That, at least, is the theory. In practice there are differences.

5.2 One approach to contract hunting

I may or may not be typical. I have been lucky enough to find a number of direct contracts over the years, and have often managed to bypass the normal contract hunting process. When I have been actively on the market, I have usually found that my contracts come not from the sources that I have approached at the time, but from unexpected directions. Nevertheless, I always follow the same approach. Whether this is the right way is open to debate, but — touch wood — it seems to work for me. I generally take these steps:

1 Contact all my earlier business contacts. This means people for whom I have worked over the years (and who can still stand the sight of me). Very often, I am happy to say, the next contract has come from there, but seldom immediately.

2 Update my c.v. with my latest experience. This process is somewhat interactive, because as I go through step 4, I find that

I need to make alterations in the light of requirements.

3   Go through the magazines and mark all the likely looking jobs. I will not work away from home, and so my search criteria are determined by type of work and geographical location.

4   Call the relevant agencies to find out more about the jobs on offer. At this stage I am almost invariably asked to send my c.v. I have this set up on my computer and use a fax package to send it (indeed, it wings its way to another agency as I type this). Since each job has a slightly different slant, and my experience is fairly varied (as is that of most contractors) I will often make changes in details on the c.v. at this stage. I always keep a computer copy of the amended c.v. so that I can refer to it when I am talking to a particular agency later. I am not talking about doctoring my c.v. to say that I have experience which I do not have, but putting a spotlight on relevant experience. For instance, I was recently working on Windows developments on Windows 3.11, Windows/NT and Windows 95, and had used MAPI (the Windows Mail API). As a result I had experience of all four. My c.v. was not particularly specific about that, and an agency phoned to ask me to highlight it, which I then did, so that her client could see where I had gained that experience.

5   Contact the agencies regularly to see what they have found.

6   The next step is — one hopes — to be offered a contract. In my experience, for some reason or other, most contracts do not come from any of steps 2–5, but from an unexpected other direction. However, I hold firmly and superstitiously to the belief that if I ignored these steps I would find myself on the scrap heap. So each time I go out on the market and actively look for work. I strongly recommend this approach — if nothing else for peace of mind.

7   Tell all the people I have contacted that I have now found a contract. This is a courtesy (and I must confess I do not always remember it). There's not point in falling out with possible future sources of work.

This approach is merely the way I do things. It has worked for me in the past, and I hope it will continue to do so. However, it is certainly not the only way. One thing I do try to do is to keep a record of who I have approached, and with what result. If you are speaking to perhaps thirty agencies, it is very easy to forget what you have said to whom. I keep a simple paper record, but, had I more time, I might well automate this. It is useful during the search process — though redundant subsequently.

One thing that I have found is that the agency who was hot last time is often all but dead the next. If you have contacted agencies during a previous job search, and they appeared to have a lot of possibilities, they are the logical ones to contact next time round. However, frequently there are new agencies around, and the old agencies change their focus, so do not be put if you receive a lot of negative responses from them. A trawl around the magazines will often yield a bunch of better contacts than approaching the same agencies again.

In many self-employed businesses (like my other jobs, singing and writing), it is useful to create a printed brochure about yourself, showing samples of your work, and summarising your experience. Though this is not necessary in computer contracting at the moment — if you have the right experience, you need only approach the agencies to find work — it should not be discounted. Particularly if you are trying to lift your business beyond just contracting into real consulting, such an approach might have a lot of merit.

The market is to a large degree a seller's market at the moment. Recently I was approached by an agency about a particular contract. She told me rather sadly that she needed to know that whoever else she put up would take the job if it was offered, because she had put two other candidates up, but, by the time the client came back with an offer, they had been snapped up by someone else. This is not unusual. Very often you will find that you will receive a bunch of offers all together. Do not be too afraid to ask a client to wait for you decision if you are not certain that the contract on offer is exactly what you want.

5.3 Sources

In the process described in the previous section, I have referred mainly to dealing with agencies. There a number of different sources for contract work, however — though agencies certainly are the most fruitful.

Newspapers

There are a number of specialist papers for computer staff — *Computer Weekly* and *Computing* being the best known. Both offer an Internet-based service as well as the normal printed version each week. Apart from articles, there are pages of job advertisements — some of which apply to contract jobs. The general strength of the market for staff can be more or less directly derived from the number of job ads in these papers — the heavier they are the more is on offer.

Computer Weekly is published by Reed Business Publishing. Details from:

Room L224, Quadrant House, The Quadrant, Sutton, Surrey SM2 5AS

Telephone enquiries: 01622 778222; Fax 0181 652 8923

Website at http://www.computerweekly.co.uk.

Computing can be obtained from:

VNU Business Publications, 32-34 Broadwick Street, London W1A 2HG

Telephone: 0171 316 9000; Fax 0171 316 9160, (to register by fax, call 0345 508796 to be faxed back a registration form)

Website at http://www.computingnet.co.uk.

As well as these general weeklies, there are magazines designed specifically for the contractor. The two main titles are the *Freelance*

Informer and the *Computer Consultant*. If you are going on the contract market it is more important that you take these magazines than any other.

The *Freelance Informer* is published fortnightly by Reed Business Publishing. Address and telephone as for *Computer Weekly*.

Website at http://www.freelanceinformer.co.uk.

Computer Consultant is published fortnightly by IP Publications. Details from:

221-233 High Street, Berkhamsted, Herts HP4 1AN

Telephone: 01442 876878; Fax: 01442 872315.

Website at http://www.computer-consultant.co.uk.

Agencies

Agencies are the most obvious source of contract work, but they vary in size and helpfulness (the two factors not necessarily corresponding).

Agencies can certainly be a most fruitful source of work. Any client looking for contractors is far more likely to go to an agency than any other source. There are a number of reasons for this. Because contractors move more frequently than other staff, they become available more quickly. Therefore, a client looking for particular skills can consult an agency, and they will then be able to search their files for suitable people. Staff with the right qualifications will be canvassed, not only on their own availability, but on whether they know other people with the same skills. They may have met them on their various assignments. Agencies advertise long lists of forthcoming and available contracts. They have a better chance of netting suitable people than individual organisations. In addition, clients can ensure that the agency has filtered out those unfortunates who do not have the right experience for the job.

Allied to the second point, many companies who are happy to advertise on their own account for full-time staff feel that it is a stigma to admit that they need to bring in contractors. They feel, perhaps, that needing such people implies poor management. This is a groundless prejudice, but hard to dispel.

Direct approaches

Some companies do recruit contractors directly, for specific projects. Often that recruitment is done via contracts already performed. It is very unusual for first-time contractors to find work in this way.

Many companies which use contractors, however, do ask other staff about their friends and acquaintances in the business. It is not unusual for a contractor to begin his career by being "headhunted" from a permanent job, because of a good reference given by a friend. Because contractors are not protected by employment law, there is less risk for employers than with full-time employees, where references can rebound, because of possible defamation of character. This is why many employers, when asked to give a reference for an ex-employee, will offer only a positive reference or none at all — though even the latter course can imply that the employer was dissatisfied.

You can find companies to contact via directories. For example, if you have a particular skill, such as knowledge of a 4GL or Case tool, you might be able to make contact with companies who use that product. If the supplier publishes a directory of users of its product (or software partners) you might be able to get hold of that and contact those people. With some skills, there is a very small and well-networked community which, if you can tap in, can provide you with all the work you will need.

Software houses

Though these are often really glorified agencies, there are some specialised software houses who regularly use contractors. The most common use of such people is to deliver teams of suitably skilled staff for particular projects. For example, a software house specialising in a particular 4GL or DBMS will often keep a list of suitably qualified contractors to approach should they land a suitable contract, rather than retaining full-time staff for that eventuality.

If you have particular skills, therefore, and wish to market them it is very sensible to find out which software houses are working in the field. Go to the software supplier in the first instance, and tell them that you are on the market. Ask them for a VAR (Value Added Reseller) list, and approach the companies on that to see if they have any work. If the product has a user group, go to meetings and tout your skills. This can be a very fruitful avenue to find work. The software house is very like an agency, but will be far more focused.

One problem with such contacts is that you may find that a software house feels the need to require a higher level of experience than would another type of agency. For instance, if you have only six intensive months of experience in a product, the software house may be reluctant to take you on — because it has to sell a high degree of competence on paper to its clients. I find that, in these circumstances, it pays to be persistent. Software houses suddenly close contracts, then need staff. Even if they have already rejected you, do not give them up. Keep yourself in front of them. Once that contract comes in, they may well need you. As long as you are confident that your experience is sufficient to do the job, you should eventually find your way in.

The Internet

There are now many Web sites and e-mail addresses from which you can find vacancies. For instance, all the computer magazines have home pages. It is very common now for contractors to have their own PCs or access to a PC with a modem, and it is very cheap to sign up with an Internet service provider, such as BT Internet or Compuserve. Almost all agencies now have a Web site, usually with a form which you can fill in if you are interested in a particular vacancy. Alternatively, a number of agencies now have World Wide Web addresses into which you can dial from an Internet session to find vacancies.

The job search facilities offered by *Computer Weekly*, *Computing*, *Freelance Informer* and *Computer Consultant* (Internet addresses above) are often all you need to find a contract. Just sign on to the site, enter some search criteria and you will be put in touch with agencies who have possible vacancies. Make sure that you have a c.v. ready to send over the Internet.

I have some problems with sending a c.v. in this way. You should have put some effort into formatting the thing to make it look neat and readable. If you are then forced to send it in text form, all that work will be lost. You could use a document format – such as MS-Office – but your recipient will not necessarily have the same package. That particular package has a different format between the 95 and the 97 version. I have tried to send HTML formatted documents, but have always been told that they are unreadable. It is a good idea to ask anybody who wants a c.v. in electronic form in what format it should be sent.

5.4 How to find the right agency

Agencies are all different, but all similar. The choice of the ideal agency for you is one of those subjective decisions which owes little to logic.

In practice, the most important thing to know is that an agency can offer a good follow-up service (see below) – paying you promptly and dealing with any problems which may arise. Your choice will be easier when you understand what you should expect an agency to do for you. If you can find people who have worked for a particular agency, get opinions from them about how well it did its job. However, at this stage, you should keep your options open. As with full-time job hunting, looking for contract work involves scanning all the advertisements for suitable-looking contracts before deciding on the right agency. The agency which you finally choose will be more likely to be determined more by the particular contract which you find than by a weighing up of the agency's pros and cons.

Not all contract jobs are advertised. Very many of them are filled from agency lists, or by the other means described. As a corollary, not all advertised contracts exist. agencies have been known to build up their portfolios by advertising non-existent jobs. Contractors or other candidates who apply are told that the job has gone "but send a copy of your c.v. anyway — for our files."

The c.v. is the key to a contractor's success, as well as a potential hazard. Its preparation is important, and it must be constantly updated, as experience is added.

A c.v. should contain a well-presented and lucid account of your career, background and personality. There are many different ways to go about preparing it. Companies who specialise in this sort of thing advise you to prepare two, a long and a short. The short is the initial "door opener", which should whet the appetite of the reader. The long has the full service history.

In practice, this approach may work — but many prospective employers will be put off by the feeling that the short c.v. has not enough detail. Particularly for contract work, this can be enough to put them off pursuing you further. Conversely, the long c.v. may be just too much to wade through. A compromise contains all the detail in a few pages. The idea, as with any selling document is to attract the prospective employer sufficiently to make him or her invite you in for an interview.

When you are preparing your c.v., you should bear in mind the type of jobs which you have seen advertised, and try to target your c.v. in those directions. For instance, if your experience is widespread, but with a preponderance of IBM AS/400 work, for which there are a lot of openings, make sure that the emphasis of the c.v. is towards such work. Lay out your experience so that it is clear that AS/400 is your target job — without throwing away the other experience. If you are going for a more general range of jobs, stress the depth and breadth of your experience. In the sample c.v. below, there is an example of a broad based target.

Figure 1: Sample c.v.

FREDDY FROG
16 Grenouille Gardens
Frogsborne
Telephone: Frogs 32655
e-mail: fred.frog@aol.com

CAREER SUMMARY

FREELANCE	1996 — present

Current Contract: **Fenestration Ltd**

Accounting system for double glazing manufacturers, written in C++ under
Windows 95. Design and development.

1994–1996   **Lion Tamers Inc**

Generalised accounting system for comic sketch writers. Written in C on IBM
PC. Designed and developed interview processing module.

1993–1995   **Aardvark International**

Ant prospecting system on IBM PC in 'C' under MS-DOS, programmer/analyst.
12 months contract was extended. System on time, "core" working and under
systems testing.

1992–1993   **Apiarists International**

Project Leader, conversion from DOS/VSE to OS/MVS, using package. No
programming involved. Project Completed on schedule. 6 months.

1991(continued)   **Acme Manufacturing**

3033 MVS/XA, analyst programmer, IMS and CICS. Installation support VTAM
system. Successfully completed. 6 months.

1990–1991   **SOG Group**

Assembler programming of transaction processor, to handle input from DEC/VAX
machines. IBM 3081 under MVS/XA. Initial 6 months, 6-month extension. Project
Completed.

1989–1990   **Allied Industries**

Analyst/Programmer – manufacturing system on Amdahl under MVS/XA, using
CICS and IMS. Language COBOL.

1986–1988   **IBM**

Trainee S.E. Working mainly in operations area, using 3033 equipment with MVS/
XA. Learnt Assembler, and COBOL.

EXPERIENCE SUMMARY

Machines:

IBM mainframes, under DOS/VSE and MVS operating systems.
IBM compatible PCs under MS-DOS, Windows and UNIX.

Languages:

Assembler: IBM (including Macro language)	5 years
COBOL	8 years
C	5 years
C++	1 year

Operating systems:

IBM MVS and DOS/VSE	8 years
MS-DOS (PC-DOS)	6 years
Windows (3.1, Workgroups and NT)	2 years

Software:

CICS	4 years
IMS	4 years
dBase	4 years
ORACLE	2 years
Uniface	1 year

Training courses:

IBM SE Workshop (Computing Systems Fundamentals)	1986
IBM 370 Basic Assembler Language	1987
IBM COBOL Language	1988
CICS programming	1988
IMS DL/I programming	1988
Analytical and Structured Techniques (Jackson)	1989
'C' programming (self paid)	1993
'C++' programming (self taught)	1995

BACKGROUND

Education:

Frognal Grammar	1976–1983
7 O levels, A levels in Physics, Maths — Pure and Applied	
Imperial College	1983–1986
Computing Science 2.1	

Born: 23 April 1965
Nationality: British
Family: Married, no tadpoles
Leisure Activities:

Photography, Motor Racing.
Computing — I have my own Pentium II based PC

Availability: One month's notice.
Current Rate: £900 per week.
Preferred Location: London and home counties

Figure 5.1 is an example of the sort of items which should be on a c.v. aimed at agencies. It ought to give an idea of the types of headings, and the level of detail needed. You should avoid being too verbose.

The section on the career to date can be expanded if there is relevant information. Whether it is arranged in ascending or descending date order is open to question. The advantage of the ascending order is that the prospective employer sees how the career has progressed, descending order gives him or her the chance easily to see the latest experience. Some agencies stress that descending order is more likely to attract, because it can very quickly show the current experience — the reader may then progress to the earlier career details if he or she wants. On balance, for contract work, descending order is probably best.

The use of a "front sheet" like this, with a career summary, means that a potential agency or employer can easily see the pertinent experience, without shuffling through pages of information. With, conceivably, hundreds of c.v.s to scan through, this can make the difference between being noticed or ignored.

The section on experience is a useful way of presenting a summary of your expertise. However, be sure to calculate accurately how much of your time has actually been spent on those skills — it should tie in with the career section. Training courses attended particularly if self-paid, gives useful information on the level of training you have had. However, if you are largely self-taught, do not be ashamed — leave training courses out if you want, your career should speak for itself.

The background section gives a potted picture of you. If you have no hobbies, don't make them up. A prospective employer may question you on them, and if he discovers that you actually know nothing about bee keeping, and spend all your time at the pub, he is unlikely to be too impressed. The last item, current rate, is somewhat contentious. I do not generally quote a particular rate, because it can be taken as a fixed item. In that case it may be too high for some prospective employers – for whom I might happily work for a lower rate – or too low for others – who might think I was not suitably high powered for them. You will have to determine a rate in the end, but it can be sensible to keep your powder dry at this stage.

There will be times when you want to avoid telling potential clients about clients with whom your relationship has been less than amicable. This is almost inevitable in the course of a career. There are a number of ways to handle this. One is simply to leave out the offending entry. This has the disadvantage that an eagle eyed company will notice it and wonder what you were doing – could you have been in prison during that time? In other words, you must have something to hide, and leaving a gap will draw attention to it.

Another way is to extend the length of the contracts around the bad one. This is untruthful, and could harm you if your potential client wants to check references and finds that you have lied about the duration of the contracts. If the contract is far enough in the past, that will probably not happen – in this case you may simply lump all the experience together in a single summary – such as "various contract jobs".

However, there is nothing wrong in coming clean. You can say something like "I terminated this contract – details on request". This will not draw criticism from your potential client, and you do not need to go into detail about the reason for the problem. It does no harm to allow a potential client to see your "soft underbelly" at times.

Preparing your c.v. is the first stage to obtaining contract work. Although the agency will probably ask you to fill in a form, this will not be the main document used. Your c.v. will find its way to all sorts of clients (see below).

5.5 Dealing with agencies

Agencies are, as has been said, a necessary part of the contracting scene. They are often criticised for their methods, and they sometimes deserve that criticism. However, they are the first and main path, for a new contractor, into the field. They also are an important factor in determining whether you will be paid promptly and efficiently, ensuring that your relationship with the client remains good, and finding you further work when the contract expires, without long delays.

Your first contact with an agency will probably be in response to an advertisement. You will have seen that they have certain types of vacancy, and will have applied. The response — almost universally — will be to ask you to send a c.v., and/or fill in an application form. They may also ask you in for an interview. All this is prior to a contract being discussed.

There have been some "cowboy" agencies. One IBM programmer, for instance, when presented with experience in Assembler under DOS/VS, was offered a contract as an OS Cobol programmer. "You can soon learn the Job Control, and I'll train you in Cobol myself". Needless to say, the contractor did not accept. Do not be taken in by such approaches.

Another activity often criticised by contractors is the sending out "blind", of c.v.s. If you have been to a number of agencies, and given them all your c.v., it can be very damaging to a prospective contract for the employer to receive the c.v. from two sources. Employers have been known to reject candidates in these circumstances, because they felt that they were spreading themselves to widely. However, even worse than this is the agency who rewrites your c.v., and fills it with factual inaccuracies. Once again, a prospective employer, reading two contradictory sets of facts about you, would be well justified in giving you a miss.

You should insist that agencies give you sight of any alterations they make to your c.v. This will help you to be presented properly, and the agency to make their sale. Even the "potted biographies", prepared by agencies to summarise your skills, should be similarly checked through, if at all possible. Whether you insist on this is up to you. Agencies can become aggressive, and point out that they have superior experience of presentation of candidates. Nevertheless, they ought to let you see what they are writing about you, in case of any material inaccuracy. This may not be practical when their résumés also include details of your references, of course.

More important still, you should tell any agency with whom you deal that, it you get wind of their sending out your c.v. without your agreement, you will immediately withdraw yourself from their list — and you should act on this. This might seem draconian, but contractors, as a group, have frequently published details of the problems which arise from these techniques.

It could be a very good idea at this stage to write to the agency with your understanding of the arrangements between you, in case of any dispute later about any of the items mentioned earlier. Some agencies will give you a standard document laying out their way of doing business — if you disagree with any of their terms, you should notify them of that in writing.

Once an agency has actually secured a contract for you, that is not the end of your relationship, rather more the beginning. After placing a candidate, assuming the employee performs satisfactorily, the agency does not see the candidate again. A contract agency, on the other hand, continues to be involved throughout.

In practice, contract agencies and full-time recruitment consultants are often the same companies. However, the recruitment consultant is paid a fee by the client (typically 15-25 per cent of first-year salary depending on the seniority and pay of the employee). The contract agency is paid on a continuous basis a percentage on top of the fee paid to the contractor.

Normally, contracts are made between the company and the agency, not the individual contractor. Your contract will be with the agency. You will fill in timesheets and have them signed by the client. These are returned to the agency, who bills the client, and pays you. The agency acts as a middle man. If you are operating a limited company, you will raise an invoice to the agency, otherwise they will pay you through a conventional payroll. Agents will normally ask for details of your company, and your VAT registration number. Although you need not register for VAT until your turnover reaches a certain figure (£49,000 in December 1997), agencies may well insist that you are registered, before accepting your freelance status.

The agency, of course, takes a cut of the amount paid by the client. This will range from 25 per cent to 50 per cent. Although some agencies freely admit how much commission they take, others — usually those who take the most — do not.

Naturally, such service charges are much criticised by contractors. If a client is paying £1,500 per week for you, it seems hard to accept that you should receive only £900. However, you do receive something for that fee. Remember that, if it was not for the agency, you would probably not have the contract. Clients do not often go out to look for contractors, as has already been established. The agency is the one who keeps tabs on contract staff, and just paying the administrative expenses of an agency and the cost of financing your contract — which may not be paid nearly as regularly by the client as the agency is paying you — will entail costs.

One area in which I find agencies to be quite infuriating is the regular follow-up call to check your availability. Once you have signed on, that is often the last you hear from them, until a few months later a lady (it is almost always a lady) calls one evening when you are in the bath, or in the middle of an argument with the children: "XYZ agency, just checking your availability". I know they may need to know this — if they are genuinely trying to place you. But in practice, very few of these general agencies ever find you anything at all. I suspect that they are just keeping the numbers on their books up to impress their clients. I apologise to all those agencies out there, but really, chaps, you should try to be a bit more focused on finding people contracts, and less on your statistics. If you have not even tried to find me a contract, do not bother me with these irritating calls, please.

During these calls, I am often asked to send an updated c.v. This, too, is quite irritating. I see no point in peppering the world with c.v.s, which will need to be updated before I next look for work, anyway. If an agency needs a c.v., it should be for sending to a prospective client. If they have previously had a c.v., they should not need that to be updated until the next contract is being sought. Therefore, agencies, please do not request c.v.s unless you are actually going to be using them.

Whatever else you do, do not let your agency down. It is true that there are plenty around, and plenty of work is available, but it is surprising how easily you can acquire a reputation for unreliability which can stick with you. This is particularly true if you have "niche" or rare skills. Always keep your agency informed about what is happening. Do not let them down unless you are absolutely unable to avoid it – and even then make sure you tell them what is happening and why. You can spoil years of carefully built-up trust by a careless action.

5.6 The interviews

There are almost always two interviews for the first contract. After that, when the agency knows you, you will probably only have to visit prospective clients. However, if you have rare skills, and an agency has a client crying out for those, he may well send you straight to the client.

You will meet a recruitment consultant at the agency offices, who will run you through a normal screening interview. The purpose of this will be to enable the agency to decide on your suitability for any of the jobs on their books, and to see what sort of candidate you are. You may be rejected at this stage — like any candidate.

The normal advice to job candidates applies. Do not approach the agency looking like the Wild Man of Borneo. Be polite, concise and as accurate as you can. Neither exaggerate nor underrate your abilities. Above all, at this stage, try to convince the agency that you will be able to represent him or her well at the client offices. It is unusual to find agencies who really understand the intricacies of the technology. However, they will have various "buzzwords" on which you must be able to satisfy them. Have you used C++ under Windows? Do you have experience of HP-UX? Have you designed general insurance systems?

Your next step, after the agency interview, is to meet the client. This is likely to be more technical, and your c.v. will be questioned. Again, try to be sober and accurate. If you make wild claims about your abilities, you will probably be caught out. Do not forget to assess the client. You may be desperate for work, but avoid committing yourself to an onerously long contract with somebody with whom you cannot possibly see eye-to-eye.

Above all, remember that you are in a sales situation. If you cannot present yourself well, and hate interviews, then contracting may not really be your forte. As a full-time employee you will do far fewer interviews, unless you change your job very often indeed.

The other important factor will be your availability. Contracts are frequently last-minute affairs. You may find yourself turned down because you cannot start tomorrow. Make sure that you contact your agency or agencies as soon as your current contract expiry date is clear. Do not leave this too long or you may have a period "resting".

However, if you are making your first sortie into the contracting world, do not make the mistake of resigning until your contract is assured. Make absolutely sure you have the offer in writing first. It would be worth turning down some short-term possibilities because you were not available in time, to avoid being unnecessarily unemployed through your own decision. (Remember that unemployment pay is not available for six weeks if you jump, rather than being pushed.)

5.7 References

Another part of obtaining a job is the supply of references. It is often hard to do this. Most people moving from job to job have the problem that they dare not name a referee until they have the job offer, because it could jeopardise their current position, but the prospective employer needs it before he or she can make such an offer. In the conventional jobs market this is not a problem, because the employer can make an offer subject to receipt of suitable references, and bad references are not very often given.

In contracting, it is slightly different. Contracts are often short, and contractors can legitimately ensure that a current client will give a reference whilst still completing a contract. References may not be necessary anyway, when you are moving from one contract to another, because the agency or software house will know what you can do. But getting that first reference may be harder, because a client will not make an offer subject to receipt of references. The normal situation is that the client needs you — preferably yesterday — but that he must not make a mistake. Therefore, if references are requested they must be instantly available, or the job may go to someone better prepared. If you are just setting out on the contract road, this can be a problem. Try to get a reference from a "friend" at your current company, in as general form as possible — addressed "to whom it may concern", rather than to a specific person — and have it available for the agency from the beginning. It may make a difference at an early stage between your being chosen, or somebody else.

5.8 Contracts

Contract negotiations

It is assumed, in this section, that we are working through an agency. Direct client-to-contractor negotiations vary somewhat. However, you will be unlikely to indulge in these unless you already have experience of agencies. If so, you will already know a fair bit about negotiations, because you will already have done a few.

Basically the negotiation of a contract is all about money. The agency will try to sell you at your rate plus their percentage. Your saleability will depend upon your level of experience and expertise. Your experience, initially will determine whether a prospective employer will even admit you for interview. Your expertise — which can only be proved on the job, or by reference — will determine whether you land the contract, and whether, once having landed it, you retain it, and even have it extended.

From the agency's viewpoint, the business is all about their margins. The higher they are, the greater the profit. They will therefore try to maximise the payment from the client, whilst minimising the payment to you. Only a very few agencies work on published margins — and even those who claim they do often cut them to be able to clinch a deal.

After a client has accepted you, they will notify the agency. The agency will then contact you. Even when you have been told by a client that you are right for the job, the agency will be involved. Their job now is to obtain the best fee. They will tell you the rate — say £800 per week. At this point, you may accept, or try to hold out for more. The agency will probably expect you to do that. You are unlikely to lose a contract if you ask for a bit more. However, if you demanded £1,200 you could expect to be told where to go.

I doubt that I am alone in being very shy about financial negotiations, and apt to blurt out too low a rate to avoid being rejected. I have more than once kicked myself (sometimes quite literally) for quoting too low, and then being accepted without question. If that happens, it is probably because the rate was below what the client expected to pay. Remember that dropping your target is usually possible, but raising it beyond what you originally quoted is far harder.

Let's say that after being told a rate of £800 you ask for £1,000. The agency will probably then say "Well, I don't know whether the client will wear that. I'll get back to them. What's the lowest you'd accept?"

At this point, you have to decide on strategy. Some people are naturals at such negotiations, most are not. If you give an answer — say £950 — the agency will almost certainly come back with an offer of that figure. If not, they will probably come back with £925. However, you might have pushed the rate up to £1,000. One answer to the question is "I'm sure you have a pretty good idea of my ideal figure, and how far the client will go." The agency may, bull-headedly, insist on knowing that figure, but, if not, you can expect to have the offer raised.

Always try to have a target figure in your own mind, below which you will not go. You may, after a number of rejections need to revise this, but it gives a starting point. Conversely, it could be too low. You can assess that by not accepting immediately any offer made — a contract in one hand, ready to sign, can be a good bargaining counter in another negotiation.

The agency will probably come back and tell you either that the client has upped its offer, or that the agency has cut its percentage. Do not believe the latter story — it is seldom true. Agents tell you such things to make you grateful. A term for it is "soft underbelly selling" — expose your soft underbelly, make the prospect feel sorry for you, and he'll be more amenable in future.

The agency may tell you that the client's offer is final. If that happens, you must decide whether the offer is reasonable — or whether it can be improved elsewhere. You should have some idea of your value. If the offer is in the correct region, acceptance may save you heartache later. An agency spurned is next to useless to you for future contracts.

Don't worry about agency rates. You are unlikely to cut them except with smaller agencies. Accept that they are a necessary evil. bigger agencies provide better security, and more efficient payment than smaller. However, the smaller firms may take more trouble with you as an individual. Many small firms are started by contractors — who therefore know the ropes, and understand your fears and worries better.

Lastly, think about expenses. If you are having to travel, or stay away from home, make sure you take this cost into consideration before agreeing a figure. Some agencies will pay expenses on top of a fee, some will want to roll the two together. However, if you have been doing a job within twenty miles of home, and the same agency asks you to commute sixty miles for the next contract, do not be afraid to ask for some additional recompense.

Do not be afraid to negotiate. Like a Turkish bazaar, in the contract business you are expected to make and accept offers, little is cut and dried.

How the contract works

Your contract will either be with the agency, or directly with the client. It will define the terms of your assignment, how long you are expected to do the work, how much you will be paid, whether expenses are due and under what terms it can be severed. Most agencies have standard terms, and, apart from checking that the terms agree with what you have negotiated, there should be little more to worry about. In practice, you are in the "cat bird seat" because you are providing the service, and are in demand. The only potential problem will be ensuring that you are paid in a timely fashion. Ideally, you should try to make sure that you are paid promptly as close to the end of the week or month — depending on the contract's terms — as possible.

Direct contracts are a little more difficult. In this case, the client may not have a standard contract for freelance workers, or, if it has, it may be inappropriate to your type of work. If you are in any doubt about it, get the contract checked by a solicitor to make sure you are not signing away your life for little or no reward. However, in today's market, if you are competent, a client will be very foolish to make your life too difficult — because you can always walk away, and your services are much in demand.

My personal view of contracts is that they are really only a statement of intent. If you end up having to dispute them, you will seldom be able to fight a legal battle against a determined opponent. I have seen people try. In one company, a contractor had previously been an employee. The company was restructuring, and had decided to be rid of him. They negotiated an attractive-seeming contract — in the terms of which was his agreement to waive his employment rights in exchange for more attractive contract terms. The company then terminated his contract within a month, so he lost both the contract and his employment rights.

He could have fought them in court, and probably won. However, he decided not to. He had seen a predecessor do the same thing, and end up with a bill for £23,000 in legal fees. That is the problem — a determined employer can always outspend a small supplier. I was cheated by the same company — but only out of three days' money. Needless to say, I did not try to fight them. There are times when it is better just to walk away.

When you have agreed your contract, you begin work with the client company. This will be very much like starting any job, you will report to a member of staff at the client's offices just like any other employee. However, if you have been introduced by an agency, you actually have two masters. The agency will nearly always be responsible for actually paying you. At the end of each week (typically), you will go to the client manager with a timesheet (normally provided by the agency). The manager will sign this, and return it to you. You will then send it to the agency. Depending upon their payment cycle (which may be weekly, fortnightly or monthly), they will pay you. If you are working via a limited company, you will enclose an invoice with the timesheet. The agency will bill the client in their turn — but this is of no direct concern to you.

Agency-contractor relations can become strained on the question of percentages taken by the agency. Letters of complaint from contractors are frequently published telling of agencies' mendaciousness. For instance, one contractor told of an agency quoting a particular rate to him — which did not seem far out of line. However, later, when his contract was not renewed, the client told him that the main reason was the cost. It turned out that the agency was actually charging 15 per cent more than they had told the contractor. This is not untypical. Larger agencies often have published structures of rates, to enable the contractor to know what is actually being paid. However, agencies are usually extremely coy about admitting the levels of their charges to their contracted staff.

Another effect of this coyness is that it is extremely hard to assess how much you, as a contractor, are worth. In Chapter 8, there is as much current information as possible on competitive rates of pay, and opportunities.

Direct contracts

You may be asked by a client to make a direct contract with them. This will avoid much of the expense, and enable you to enjoy a higher rate of pay. Cutting out the middle man is an attractive concept. However, there are a number of important reasons why this can be dangerous.

If the client has been introduced to you via an agency, they will expect at the least an introduction fee. This will normally be based on your salary in a full year. If the client is not prepared to pay this, he is likely to be in breach of contract. the only person who is likely to suffer is you yourself. You may find yourself blacked by the agency, and rumours about your unreliability may spread.

Clients can also do naughty things to you. Some years ago, a contractor fell foul of such a situation. He was working on contract for a company, and offered a full-time job by their systems manager. He then turned down a contract which he had verbally accepted. He knew that this was dangerous, because he would upset the agency. The client company's personnel department were telephoned by the agency and told the story — with some embellishments. As a result, against the assurances of the systems manager, he was told that there was no job for him after all. He was actually paid a month's salary for the trouble, and learnt a very salutary lesson.

You could certainly argue that he should have got a firm written offer before turning down the other contract — with the benefit of hindsight, that was true — but it is not always so easy when you are in the heat of negotiation. In this case, the company involved was a household name, so he believed, mistakenly as it turned out, that promises would be kept.

Nevertheless, direct contracting can be very much more profitable, and satisfying. If you find that you work well with a company, and that an initial contract of, say, three months is likely to run and run, and if that client is prepared to pay off the agency so that everybody is happy, then you are fortunate indeed. Normally the agency will need either a full year's commission, or the assurance of their being used to recruit other staff. As long as your client will do this, you should be safe enough.

Lastly, you can consider looking for contracts without the use of an agency. This is something you should really only do after you have experience of contract work through an agency. The main problem is then to find a suitable contract. Unless you are known to a company, you are unlikely to do that, without an enormous amount of effort. You may strike lucky — or you may come to realise why agencies charge such high fees.

Length of contracts

Contracts have to be of a certain duration. The shortest are one month or less, the longest are measured in years. When you are looking for a contract, you must be prepared to tell the agency what sort of length you require. This will be important, since it will tell them which companies to approach.

How you decide what sort of contract is best for you depends on many factors. If you are contracting so that you can take the summer off next year, a long contract is undesirable. Similarly, if you are intending to move house in a few months and are merely looking for a "fill-in" until that time, you will not want a long contract.

Many contracts start off relatively short, but then extend. It is not at all unusual to find contractors who have worked with a company for longer than many of its full-time employees. In some ways these can defeat the object of contracting — why not join the company full-time? However, if, for instance, you need flexibility, such a contract can be a very comfortable arrangement.

When a contract comes near to its end, you often have two choices. The first is to find another contract — or full-time job. The second is to extend your contract.

Not all contracts, by any means, are extendible. However, many are, and if you are happy with your current client, you may well fell happy to stay on that contract. The only thing to think about is whether you should, at the same time, try to negotiate an increase in rate.

If you are not extending your current contract, be sure to let the agencies know when you will next be available. One of the main controls which agencies have is to keep lists of contract staff availability. You will probably be approached when your contract is nearing its end as a matter of course.

Even in recessionary times, there are quite a few contracts available. If you have the right skills, you should be able to choose the right length for you. However, do not be surprised if, having started a contract you end up becoming a fixture at the client site.

5.9 Other ways to sell your skills

If you are a more senior contractor — in the consultant category — you might consider producing a more marketing oriented brochure about yourself, to use as a mailshot. This could include details about your "portfolio" of skills, and about other skills to which you have access. For example, though you yourself may not be up-to-date in, say, Sybase development, you might be able to call on a colleague who is. In that case, you can offer access to that skill to a potential client. If you also encourage your colleagues to sell skills that you can offer in the same way, you can extend the possibilities available to you.

6 Finance

6.1 Introduction

Before I start this section, I must give a warning. Do as I say, not as I did. I got into a royal mess personally through trusting somebody close to me, who proved to be a liar and a cheat. *Always* make sure that *you* are in control of your own affairs, do not leave matters to others, however much you may trust them, because, ultimately, it is your own responsibility to ensure that everything is legal and correct, and you who pay if it is not.

It has already been stressed that professional advice should be sought in matters arising from company formation, self-employment and the myriad decisions which you will need to make.

For reasons already given, the best person to advise in these matters is an accountant. You will need to have one anyway, and accountants have sufficient legal knowledge on company matters to give good advice there too. If you arrive at the point where you need more than an accountant can do, you are in a sorry plight indeed. Indeed, solicitors frequently have to defer to accountants on matters of company law, unless they are from the most expensive, corporate, firms.

The computer contractor has in the past been singled out by the Inland Revenue as a suitable case for doubt. Like many freelance staff, there has been talk of changing their status so that even the protection afforded by a legitimate limited liability company would be denied. Presumably this is because of the huge sums which can be earned in our industry. For this reason, if for no other, you need to ensure that you fully understand your position, and act at all times strictly according to the rules.

In this section, some advice will be given. However, it should be stressed that detailed accounting advice is outside the scope of this book. For such advice, please refer to your accountant, or to one of the many books written on the subject.

6.2 Preparation

Prior to searching for a contract, you must make sure that you can operate your life in this new mode. Remember that there will be lean times — particularly between contracts — and that these can impose a financial strain on you and your family. Make sure that your spouse both understands and agrees with this.

Just because you are becoming a contractor does not mean that you have to go out and buy yourself lots of gear — such as computers, answering machines, mobile phones and photocopiers. You must plan your acquisitions. If you are working at client sites most of the time, do you need a high powered computer of your own? How often will you actually need to use a photocopier — if not that often, a photocopy shop will prove far cheaper. You should certainly consider having a mobile phone if you are travelling around a lot — but it can be hard to answer it and negotiate your next contract when you are sitting in a client's office. I have found that answering machines are somewhat unreliable — it is easy to forget to switch them on when the last person leaves home. A good alternative is the British Telecom answering service, which costs £4.65 per quarter and makes sure that all calls are answered. The only disadvantage is that, if you are working away from home, you cannot phone in from outside and retrieve your messages.

Another consideration is your car. Typically, as a contractor, you will be travelling to work by car for at least a portion of your journey. Is that old banger of yours really reliable enough? Should you consider replacing it — and, if so, can you afford it? I have had problems with old cars throughout my working life. If you are in full-time employment, you can get away with being late occasionally because of a breakdown, but, as a contractor, your income relies on your getting to work on time every day. Also, if you do break down, you will then have to take time off to take the car to be fixed, and that, too, will cost money in lost working time. Before you make a move, consider, if you need to use your car to get to your clients, whether it is reliable enough. If not, replace it — if you can afford to — or wait until you can.

Make sure that you have set up your personal affairs before you start — in this chapter we will discuss the work an accountant will do for you. It is sensible to set these things up before you start the actual work. However, many agencies will help you with such things — introducing you to an accountant who, in turn, will set up the whole package for you.

6.3 Government bodies

When you run a small business, you are under a number of obligations. A company can be any size from a one-man band to a multi-national. The government still tend to treat you as if you were ICI, expecting you to devote an enormous amount of time to form filling and reporting — with the direst threats should you make a mistake. Forms — with some exceptions — are couched in arcane language, and often different terminology is used by different departments to describe the same thing. You are under an obligation to keep records, and the various departments (HM Customs and Excise, the DSS and Inland Revenue) can all insist on coming and scrutinising these. It all seems rather daunting — and very much an interference with normal business life.

However, in their defence I should say that, when one or other department makes a "control visit" to check your books, they are extremely polite and positive. I have had Customs and Excise and DSS visits, and the people involved could not have been more helpful, polite and positive. They give the impression — a genuine one, I believe — that they are there to help, not to punish. If they find errors, they point them out politely, and allow you leeway — within reason — to correct them. As long as you are playing straight with them, they are very straight with you. So, do not be frightened of them, but do all you can to keep all your records tidy and accurate.

One problem I have found with government departments is that, when it comes to a dispute, they listen far more seriously to a qualified person than to a private individual. For instance, if you are invited to a meeting with Customs and Excise to discuss a problem, it is best to bring your accountant along. Indeed, if you try to set up such a meeting on your own, you may find it impossible — whereas your accountant can usually be more persuasive. Even if you know precisely the arguments, and can answer all the questions, the Civil Service will often not be as prepared to deal with you as with your professional adviser. It is probably common sense — though it can be frustrating.

6.4 Finding your accountant

Where can you go to find a suitable accountant, and what should you be looking for? Since the professions were allowed to advertise in 1985, many accountancy and legal firms have taken the opportunity of setting up their stalls by advertising on television, and other media.

However, the sort of companies who can afford such marketing are unlikely to be suitable for the individual contractor. What you will need is a relatively small, cheap firm, with experience of your kind of trade, who can also be relied upon to give correct advice.

This is not a particularly easy combination to find. Small firms are ten-a-penny. The Yellow Pages, local Chamber of Commerce directories and magazines have a plethora of lists of accountants. Finding the right one for you may be more difficult.

The contracting trade papers (see Chapter 5) always carry advertisements for companies which specialise in accounting for contractors. They usually offer a complete service — including the setting up of your limited company, doing all necessary returns and dealing with the authorities on your behalf. Contact some of these — they will usually send you a pretty helpful brochure describing their services.

Recommendations are obviously a good start. If you have friends in a similar field who have a good accountant, go and talk to him or her. Your agency will often put you in contact with somebody. If you trust them, they will usually be able to recommend somebody with specific experience of computer contracting.

As has already been said, a big firm will probably not be any more use to you than a small one. Big companies have big fish to fry. Whatever they may tell you, an account which will yield them, at best, £2,000 per annum is not worth having. Their charges will be significantly higher than the small firm anyway, because they have high overheads. Since "professionals" charge by the hour, you will get considerably less bang for your buck with a large than with a small firm.

Set against that, however, is the apparent higher risk with a small, unknown company. At least a large company appears to offer sufficient expertise to ensure that disasters do not happen. However, in practice this may not actually be so. If you go to a big company, you will almost certainly be dealt with by a junior who is, in effect, a trainee — whatever qualifications he or she may sport. This is not a bad thing — everybody has to start somewhere. However, you may feel that trainees should cut their teeth on other people's problems and that you need mature, experienced advice. With a smaller company, you are more likely to be dealt with by a more experienced person. Even so, whereas a larger firm's senior will delegate down to a qualified junior, a smaller company will only have non-qualified "articled" juniors if work is passed down. In these circumstances, you may find that you have no help at all if serious problems, needing experience, arise.

Therefore a safe option is to look for a small to medium sized company. You should then ask the representative what resources they have to deal with your business. Can they assure you that they will personally be available to advise? Who will actually do the audit? What are the firm's cost scales— and do they apply to help even if given by a junior?

When you have found a suitable firm, be sure to get references from some of their clients — preferably in the same business. Ask whether they have experienced difficulties in getting attention on both run-of-the-mill and urgent matters. If they have experienced delays, have these cost them extra money? There will inevitably have been problems, but have these been satisfactorily dealt with? Has the cost been as predicted at the beginning? What extra services have been offered and used (like personal advice, insurance assistance, legal help)?

My previous accountant was very helpful in these matters. As I have hinted, my affairs have not been particularly simple. He helped me to set up the most tax-efficient system for my company's accounts, and — in the past — to minimise my accounting costs. I paid a monthly fee to him to spread the cost of his bill over the year. He helps me to prepare my year-end returns. Officially an audit is no longer necessary for small businesses, but you still need an accounting statement, which is best prepared by an accountant. Since my affairs are quite straightforward these day, I am moving to a fixed price firm who will do the whole job for me at a far lower cost.

Other types of accounting firm

There are now many specialists in this business who provide services to contractors. Companies such as SJD, JSA and Lawrence Grant — whose details appear in the *Freelance Informer* — provide specialist services to contractors. These may be general accounting or complete "facilities management" services. In the latter case, all you need do is send timesheets to the company, and they will raise invoices, and do all your accounting for you — paying you as an employee. They charge a fee to do this work, but it is usually a fixed amount per month.

This is an attractive option if you are dipping your toe into the contracting stream, and do not expect to continue for long, or if you want to avoid the chores associated with running a small business. Another advantage of letting such a company take the burden is that they will often pay you on a regular basis – even when your invoices are not yet paid. They also have more "clout" than you as an individual would have, when it comes to chasing clients for payment. This is similar to commercial factoring – however, that is usually charged as a percentage of your invoice value, rather than a fixed fee.

Some agencies operate these services – but if you use one, make sure that all the correct returns are being made, or you might end up with a problem with the authorities.

Note that, with the abolition of ACT in 1999 (see ACT and Corporation Tax, page 108), you must be a little circumspect in your choice of accountant. A large firm who operate a "factory" style service, where they do all the work for you and another 2,000 contractors, may find it difficult to assemble your year-end figures in time to meet the deadline for payment of June 1st of the following tax year. If they do not, you will be liable to pay interest on the outstanding balance. This could be quite a substantial sum. When you are choosing your accountant, make sure that you check that he can meet this deadline.

6.5 Running your accounts

Once you have found an accounting firm, you must work with them. They should tell you how they want you to report to them. You really only need them to rubber-stamp your accounts, and advise you on which expenses you can claim against tax. For the accounting firms, such jobs are often known as "brown paper parcels". The client sends in copies of invoices, receipts and loads of expense slips for the accountant to unravel and sort into a form suitable for preparing year-end accounts — all in a large brown envelope. The more organised you are in preparation of these pieces of paper, the cheaper will be your audit.

You will need to set up books of accounts, to record the financial transactions which your company will undertake. Even if you are trading as an individual, you will need to record this information. Broadly speaking, you should only need one ledger, to record all income and expenditure. Alongside that you should keep evidence of all claims, in the form of invoices raised by and against the company, and receipts for miscellaneous expenditure. These should be recorded in your ledger. In a later section, we will cover how you should set up that ledger — with your accountant's advice.

In practice, you can usually run your business on a very simple "cash received" basis. This means that you keep a cash book which records all income and outgoings in relation to the business. You can be a bit more elaborate if, for instance, you are purchasing software or hardware to help you with your business on a regular basis — but you are unlikely to need to run a full sales, purchase and nominal ledger system.

The format of the ledger itself is best discussed with the accountant, who will advise on the layout and headings which would be best for your accounts, so that he can perform an audit at the minimum cost. Broadly speaking, you should keep two sections, one for income, the other for expenditure. All transactions should be recorded in the appropriate section, and totalled up. If you raise or receive credits (for instance for defective goods, or over-invoicing) these should be recorded in the same section as the original invoice. They should be the only entries with a reversed or negative sign on the sheet.

If you are registered for VAT — and many agencies insist on this — you must keep a record of the invoice numbers and invoice dates (known as "tax points"). It is advisable to do this anyway in your ledger. You will need to make regular VAT declarations to the Customs and Excise, along with payments. Your accountant will advise you on precisely how best to keep these records, and other aspects of VAT. A sample VAT invoice format is shown in Figure 6.1. Note that you should keep an accurate register of invoice numbers. Even where an invoice is cancelled, it should be recorded. Breaks in invoice number sequence may be carefully investigated.

If you are VAT registered, you must quote a valid VAT number, and account for VAT collected (see page 111). If you have a company, its registered number should appear on the invoice. Some larger companies insist on your quoting their purchase order number, if they have one. It is wise to make sure that you fulfil all their criteria – failure to do so for any reason will merely give them an excuse to avoid payment. It is also a good idea to put down your terms of payment. Companies almost invariably set their own – whatever their agreement may be with you, but it is your choice whether you accept this. Normally agencies pay thirty days in arrears (and this is often written into the contract). If you quote those terms, it is quite acceptable to chase them if the payment has not been received after that time. Note that it is not normal to charge interest on overdue invoices – though there are moves to make it easier to do so.

If you are running your own company, you will also have to administer the payroll. This will involve acquiring the relevant tables from the Inland Revenue, and using these to calculate the correct income tax and National Insurance payments. This will be covered in more detail in the section on Taxation and payments, page 100.

The final result of all the work is to create a set of papers which represent the company's trading position at the end of the year. This will be used to determine how much Corporation Tax is payable by the company. With the current government, Corporation Tax is running at a lower level than income tax, unless you are on a high level of earnings. A major advantage of the use of a limited company (apart from the limitation of liability) is that it enables you to claim some expenses against Corporation Tax.

Spawning systems Ltd
16 Grenouille Gardens, Frogsborne
Tel: Frogs 32655

INVOICE

United Apiarists Limited	INVOICE NUMBER	008
Bee Hive	DATE AND TAX POINT	10 January 1999
Honeypot Lane	YOUR PO NUMBER:	FG800868
Beresford		

To: five days @£200 per day in week ending 10 January 1999	1,000.00
Net	1,000.00
Vat @ 17.5%	175.00
Invoice total	**1,175.00**

Terms: Due on receipt of invoice

VAT No 625 9999 99

Registered in England No: 99999999

Figure 6.1: Sample VAT Invoice Layout

6.6 Accounting systems

Do you need a computer system to keep track of all this? Personally, I do not think so. A good spreadsheet is quite adequate. All you really need is a set of ledger sheets, and a summary (see, for example Figure 6.2 and Figure 6.3).

Sales information

This details all the invoices you raise and should be kept in a ledger sheet such as that shown below in Figure 6.2. If you are paying VAT on a cash-received basis (i.e., you only pay VAT to HM Customs & Excise when you have been paid yourself – rather than when you raise the invoice, see page 112), you should also show when an invoice has been paid.

Invoice date	Inv No	To:	Details:	Gross Amount	Net Amount	VAT	Date paid	Remarks

Figure 6.2: Sample Sales Ledger Sheet

You might also need to show your client's purchase order number – if clients normally use these. The Remarks column is useful if you want to record some further information – such as when you have chased the customer for payment. This can also be recorded, if you are using a spreadsheet program, as a note appended to the column. In this way, it does not clutter the ledger sheet.

Purchases and expenses

A second sheet should be kept detailing payments made by the company. This should show the same details as your sales ledger sheet (see Figure 6.3), but there should also be a way to allocate the cost to a particular expenditure category for analysis. Such an analysis might include headings for purchase of Computer Equipment, Software, Telephone etc.

Invoice date	Inv No	To:	Details:	Gross Amount	VAT	Net Amount	Date paid	Analysis columns	...

Figure 6.3:Sample Purchase Ledger Sheet

You should keep full details of all items you intend to claim as expenses, and of all payments made against those items. Since you will be reclaiming VAT against some of these items, there should be a column for that.

Accruing funds

You will typically have three sorts of tax to pay each quarter (though, as I have said, those quarters are not necessarily synchronised with one another): VAT, income tax and National Insurance and Advanced Corporation Tax (ACT). In addition, at the end of the year you will have to pay some Corporation Tax.

I find it most useful to move money into a deposit account, as soon as it is received from my clients, to cover these costs — so that it never becomes part of my normal spending money. That way I never (or seldom) have unexpected surprises — like finding that I have to overdraw to pay a tax bill.

6.7 Taxation and payments

Introduction

There's nothing so sure as death and taxes. However much we may dislike them, we have no option but to pay. However, you are certainly not obliged to maximise the amount you pay and you are entitled to mitigate their effect in a number of ways. However, whilst such tax avoidance is perfectly legitimate, tax evasion — the non-payment of taxes which are due — is certainly not. Evading tax is illegal, and carries heavy penalties. If the Inland Revenue suspect you of such activities, they will be extremely diligent in investigating your affairs

— indeed the only department more diligent is the Ministry of Agriculture if they suspect you of putting agricultural diesel in your private car!

The whole subject of taxation is complex, and, unless you are absolutely confident that you understand what you are doing, it is essential to take an accountant's advice. Apart from anything else, the law changes year by year, and only an expert can keep up with it. Also, accountants, who are dealing with the authorities on a daily basis will be more likely to have their views and figures accepted than an unqualified individual.

Running a limited company may be the most attractive option from the agencies' standpoint — it protects them from the unwelcome attentions of the Inland Revenue and DSS. However, although the most popular form of self-employment, it is still expensive. The employer's National Insurance contribution is a form of "job tax" which costs a lot of money. Most contractors get around these problems in a variety of ways. The first is to employ somebody else — your wife or grown-up children — to spread the load. This can allow you to take advantage of their tax allowances, and will reduce your own tax liabilities at the higher rate. Another is to pay part of your income through the use of dividends. These can be paid during the year in lump sums. If you intend to do this, speak to your accountant. He must be told about each payment, and he or you will fill in a return to the Inland Revenue for Advanced Corporation Tax (ACT). This return is cumbersome and complex.

In this section, I will deal with tax and methods of payment. However, I must stress that I am not an accountant, and what I am writing is intended for your guidance, not as an instruction. You must consult a qualified accountant for advice. He will be able to tell you how feasible it is to operate in the way I describe, and what the current feeling is in official circles. When your company is registered, you will receive a bundle from the Inland Revenue with instructions on calculating income tax and national insurance. You may well decide not to bother with this yourself, but to leave the whole thing to your accountant.

I have tried to give a flavour of the tasks involved in running PAYE, ACT and VAT. Though these are cumbersome systems, if you can program a computer or design systems, you should certainly be able to administer accounts, they are not beyond you. I make no apologies for going into quite a lot of detail.

Income tax

You will almost certainly elect to pay yourself and any other associates a salary, on which income tax and National Insurance will be payable. Income tax is the most familiar form of taxation. It is based upon a rate of 20 per cent (at the time of writing) paid on the first £4,100, 23 per cent paid on the next £22,000 and 40 per cent on anything over £26,100. You are given some personal allowances on which tax is not payable. The basic allowance is £4045 plus £274.50 for a married person. You are also allowed relief on mortgage interest on borrowings up to £30,000. This is allowed at the lower rate of 15 per cent in 1997/98 and 10 per cent in 1998/99.

This is all quite complicated. Actual calculations are made on a pro-rata basis. The way it works is that your total income in a year to date is multiplied up to deduce what it would have been for the whole year. The tax is then calculated (after deduction of allowances). That figure is then reduced by the same factor. The tax you have already paid in the year is then subtracted to give a figure for the tax due in this period. The factor applied is simply the number of months in the year divided by the number of the current month (if you are paid on a monthly basis, otherwise the number of weeks). You will be pleased to hear that you do not have to do that calculation.

The Inland Revenue publish tables to help you. These will be sent to you when you register your company along with a set of help sheets to guide you through the maze. For your income tax calculations two tables are used. The first is used to calculate how much tax-free pay you have in the period, the second is used to calculate the tax payable.

You tax-free pay is based on your tax code. If you are a single person, with a single person's allowance, you might have a tax code of 404L. Assume you pay yourself monthly at a rate of £2,000 per month, and you are now calculating your tax for month 5 (6th August to September 5th). Tax codes consist of a number either prefixed by or suffixed with a letter. Alternatively they may be simply a letter code. There are two letter codes — BR and NT. BR means that tax is to be deducted at basic rate, without any tax-free allowances. NT means that no tax is to be deducted. It is unlikely that you will fall into either category.

Assuming that yours is a normal tax code, first you go to your Pay Adjustment Table (known as "Table A"). This table does not alter from year to year, or when tax rates are changed, since it is used merely to show how much tax-free pay you have in a period. In Table A, you look at the entry in month 5 for code 404. This is £1,687.10. You must first do the calculations shown in Table 6.1.

Table 6.1: Taxable Pay Calculation

Pay in month:	2,000.00
Previous pay to date	8,000.00
Total Pay to date	10,000.00
Less free pay	1,687.10
Total Taxable Pay to Date	8,312.90

If your tax code is prefixed by a letter D, or the tax office tells you to work on a "week 1, month 1" basis, you should always use the week 1/ month 1 entry in Table A. If you have a D prefix, you are not entitled to any pay adjustment. If it starts with a K, you should make an adjustment by adding the figure for Additional Pay from the Pay Adjustment tables, rather than subtracting free pay.

Now you must work out what tax should be paid on that amount. You do this by using the other set of tables — Taxable Pay Tables ("LR + B to D"). These are re-issued whenever the tax rates are altered.

First see which table to use. The tables at the front of the booklet let you do this. In our example, we look at the entry for month 5 and see that our amount (£8,312.90) does not exceed the figure in column 2 (£10,875), but does exceed that in Column 1 (£1,709) so we need to use table B.

We now go to table B, to find the nearest round figure below 8,312. This is 8,300. The remainder after subtracting this from 8,312 is 12. We do the calculation as shown in Table 6.2.

Table 6.2:
Tax Due
Calculation

		Figure	Tax due
		8,300	1,886.00
		12	2.76
	Total	8,312	1,888.76

Now, we must subtract an amount to compensate for the lower rate of tax (20 per cent on the first £4,100). This is shown on the same page as £51.25 in month 5.

Thus the total tax due to date is 1,888.76 minus 51.25 = £1,837.51.

In the previous month, we will have paid tax to date on £6,650.32 of £1,488.50. You should therefore pay tax of £349.01 this month.

The Inland Revenue expects you to put these results on a deductions working sheet, known as a P11. I use a spreadsheet, and then transpose the information over to the P11.

Income tax and National Insurance are payable monthly, on the 19th of the following month. However, if your average monthly payments are less than £600 you can elect to pay quarterly — by notifying the Collector of Taxes. Payments are made using a pre-printed paying in book. No returns are made to the Inland Revenue during the year.

At year end you will have to fill out forms to summarise payments made in the year. This form is called a P14 — and uses the same column headings as the P11. In addition, you will have to fill out an end of year summary form (P14), employer's annual return (P35) and employees' certificates of pay, income tax and National Insurance contributions (P60) for everybody who has been paid. The latter is at the back of the P14 form.

National Insurance

Whoever thinks that civil servants are literally that, has not had to deal with PAYE systems. For some reason or other, National Insurance is levied in a completely different way from income tax — though both are paid together. If anybody out there with any influence reads this, can you please do away with this hideously complicated system and combine the two?

National Insurance, for employees, is worked out based purely on a percentage of pay. There is an amount to pay for the privilege of employing somebody (in this case, probably yourself) and an amount which the employee must pay. These are percentages based on monthly or weekly earnings at a particular time, which are "banded". The resulting figures are then tabulated in a much simpler form than those income tax tables.

Assume that you are not a "contracted out" employee (you are, believe me), paid £2,000 per month. To calculate your National Insurance contributions, you go to National Insurance tables and pick up the figures from the monthly table. There are three columns:

1a is the column showing employee's earnings on which "contributions" (they make it sound like a pleasure!) are payable. You pick the next lowest figure to the one you are paying.

1b shows the total which must be paid to HMG

1c shows the amount which is to be paid by the employee

In our example, these figures are shown as £1,997, £378.28 and £178.28. You will pay £378.28 to the government.

It is interesting to see the effect of National Insurance payments. The first is that, for middling incomes, because of the employer's contribution (which ranges from 3 per cent to 10 per cent) to which you add the employee's contribution (ranging from 2 per cent to 10 per cent), you will probably pay more National Insurance than income tax. This is academic in some ways — it all goes into the same gaping hole. However, if there were a legitimate way to reduce this figure, you could significantly reduce your tax burden.

The second effect is that lower-paid people pay far less National Insurance in proportion than they do income tax. Indeed, below £278 (in 1998/99), they pay none at all. Note that this figure is exact; if you pay a person £278 per month, you will have to pay National Insurance — on £277.99, you will not. This is an example of a "poverty trap".

Thus, if you can arrange to be paid a modest salary, but to receive other money in some other way, you can significantly reduce your tax burden. If you can arrange that other people (such as your wife or partner) who help in running your business are paid less than £278, you can escape paying any National Insurance payments for them at all. This is not tax evasion, it is perfectly legitimate. I have had a National Insurance inspection, and they did not bat an eyelid about it.

Though it is separate from income tax, National Insurance is paid using the same paying in book as income tax, and the only return done is the same annual return.

Dividends

So, how do we do reduce National Insurance liabilities? The answer is simple, by paying dividends to shareholders. Your limited company is set up with a certain number of shares (typically 100). These represent the capital put into the company in the first place. In fact the whole arrangement is fairly irrelevant for these purposes — since you yourself are the company. However, some of these shares can be owned by other people — such as your spouse or partner. As a shareholder, you and your fellow shareholders are then entitled to a share of the profits of the company in proportion to their shareholdings. Payments made to shareholders are subject to Advanced Corporation Tax (ACT) instead of income tax or National Insurance. This system will end in 1999 – after which you will have to accrue corporation tax to be paid in the month of June following the end of the tax year in question.

If your company is invoicing at the rate of £4,000 per month, and you pay it all out to yourself in salary (with no expenses or other costs allocated), you will incur employer's National Insurance on the first £2,015 of £201.50. Take this as a yearly figure (£2,418), and you will have £45,582 remaining to pay yourself in salary. If you push this figure through the self-assessment software provided by HMG (see self-assessment later in this chapter), you will see that the total income tax and National Insurance due would be £12,490.80 for a married person with no other allowances. Add to this the employer's National Insurance figure of £2,418, and you will pay a total tax bill of £14,638.80.

As we said at the beginning of this chapter, nobody is obliged to maximise the amount they pay to the government in taxes. If you have a spouse or partner who is not working for anybody else, and who has a proportion of shares in your company – say 50 per cent, you can work things differently.

Firstly, you should pay him or her a salary of £277.99 per month. This will not attract National Insurance. You can pay yourself the same amount, if you wish – and that will not attract National Insurance either. In practice, it is probably better to pay yourself a rather more realistic figure – if only to ensure that your credit-worthiness is maintained. But let us stick to that figure for now. The monthly amount you would have to distribute as a dividend (assuming no other expenses) would be £3,440. This would be distributed equally between you, as a gross annual dividend of £20,640 each. On this you would pay ACT (see below) of 20 per cent – and the company would make up an additional 1 per cent in

Corporation Tax after the end of the tax year. In total the tax payable by each person would be 21 per cent of £41,280 – or £8,669.

Assuming you paid yourself and your spouse at a similar rate throughout the year, and that you had normal tax codes, you would each earn £3,335.88 in salary and £20,640 in gross dividends – not quite entering the 40 per cent tax threshold. On this you would each have paid £4,335 in ACT. Once again, I am assuming that every penny paid to the company was paid to you or your spouse and it incurred no deductible expenses.

Under this system, your total tax bill would be £8,669. You would save yourself nearly £6,000 in tax. I must again stress that this is not illegal. It is tax avoidance not evasion and completely legitimate.

However, you should not pay dividends unless you have profits in the company. This is not usually a problem with contractor's companies, which do not amass large debts. However, remember that you must take into account the future liability to pay tax when you are calculating how much profit you have available for payment of dividends.

ACT and Corporation Tax

As was mentioned in the earlier section, if you pay yourself and your fellow shareholders periodic dividends, you become liable to Advanced Corporation Tax (ACT). The ACT system is run by the Inland Revenue. It is to be abolished in April 1999, but until then, the system remains.

ACT is payable on fixed quarter days throughout the year – the periods being based on the calendar quarters January to March, April to June, July to September and October to December. In addition, if your company's tax year does not fall on one of these quarter dates, you must make another return on the last day of that tax year – i.e. you will make five payments per annum.

Well before the end of each quarter, you, or your accountant, will receive an ACT form (known as a "CT61") from the Inland Revenue with a payslip. ACT must be paid within fourteen days of the end of a return period.

ACT is, at the time of writing, 20 per cent. This means that, if you vote a dividend of, say, £2,500, you will pay 20 per cent — £500 — to the government in tax. The dividend is thus reduced to £2,000. That is simple enough, but the way it is described on the ACT form is as arcane as you would expect from a Civil Service which, despite the protestations of politicians, is very reluctant indeed to make things easy for small businessmen. The way they work is to say that the sum of £2,000 is the "distribution" (logical enough), to which you must apply tax by dividing by 4 to calculate the "ACT payable". You then add the sums together to get back to what anybody else would call the dividend — but which for some reason (buried in the past) is called a "franked payment". Mathematicians among you will recognise that this is the same thing (20 per cent off a gross sum gives the same amount as 25 per cent of the resultant net sum) — but every time I fill in a CT61 I have to think very carefully about what I am doing.

There are many other boxes on the ACT form relating to dividends paid in other ways on which tax has been paid. In most cases these figures will not be relevant to you. If they are, your accountant really ought to be filling in the form for you.

The other thing you must bear in mind when paying yourself by dividends is that you should accrue or save up some money for the balance of tax which will be payable at the end of the year. The way it works is that, as a shareholder in a limited company, you are entitled to dividends voted on profits. These must be paid in the form of ACT, but, unless you are a higher rate taxpayer, you personally will not have to pay any more tax on that income. However, the rate of Corporation Tax for small businesses is now (in July 1998) 21 per cent per annum — reduced from 23 per cent. Therefore, although you have no personal need to pay any more tax, your Company must make up the balance. That is payable nine months after the end of the company's financial year. Therefore you should accrue this additional sum.

Dividend payments are the most common way of offsetting income tax liabilities for contractors. It was expected that the ACT system would be abolished by the new Labour government, but, instead, the Chancellor initially reduced the rate of corporation tax — making it more beneficial to pay dividends, but retained ACT. The abolition of ACT was announced in the second budget.

Once ACT is abolished, you will have to accrue all your Corporation Tax liability, instead of paying it in four chunks during the year, and a smaller chunk after the end of the tax year. This will be beneficial — in that you can earn interest on the money while it sits in your bank. However, you must avoid the temptation to dip into that account to ease cash flow. You will be in trouble if you cannot find the Corporation Tax at the right time.

A big advantage of using dividends is that you can spread the load of payments among shareholders (most often family members). As long as the net payment in dividends does not take their income into the higher rate tax bracket, they will be able to be paid without income tax or National Insurance being levied. If the total payments take you or them into the higher tax bands, tax at the difference between the Corporation Tax rate of 20 per cent and the income tax rate of 40 per cent will be charged. This means that the dividend route is not particularly attractive to higher rate tax payers — though there is still a saving in National Insurance.

The disadvantage of the dividend route is that you will find yourself unable to set aside so much for pension, the maximum for which is based on your taxable income. However, you will be drawing money at a lower net rate of tax, and will not be paying National Insurance payments against that income. You should consult your accountant or a financial adviser for the most effective mix between salary and dividends — to maximise your pension payments. This calculation will depend on your age, your expected retirement age and the amount of pension you desire.

VAT

VAT is a net tax on the value added to the supply of goods or services. If your turnover exceeds £49,000 you should register for VAT. In practice, it is sensible for all contractors to register — since many companies will not deal with non-registered people. Moreover, if you are registered, you can claim back VAT on purchases made legitimately on behalf of your company. The way it works is very simple (far simpler than income tax, National Insurance and Corporation Tax).

Any bill you raise will have added to it VAT at the current rate (now 17.5 per cent). This will be applied to all items on that bill. This applies even to expenses — even where they have VAT on them already. In that case the gross sum claimed (a hotel bill, for instance) will have VAT applied on top. If you purchase items for use by the company, on which VAT is levied, that tax can be offset against VAT which you have charged your customers. That's all there is to it.

The VAT system is fairly simple, and Customs and Excise are now reasonably helpful to small businesses. All you have to do is fill in a quarterly return and send it, with your payment, to your local VAT office. When you register for VAT, that office will contact you. They will send you the return each quarter, leaving you a month after the end of your VAT quarter to return it. Your VAT quarter is based on your financial year — so you have to fill out four returns each year.

Note that it is your responsibility to account for VAT correctly. You may appoint an agency to do it, but, if they do it wrong, it is your responsibility to clear up the mess.

A VAT return has only nine figures to fill in, and three of these are likely to be zero (unless you work overseas). A VAT return looks like Figure 6.4

Figure 6.4:
VAT Return

		£	p
Vat due in this period on sales and other outputs	1	3678	88
Vat due in this period on acquisitions from other EC Member States	2		00
Total VAT due (the sum of boxes 1 and 2)	3	3678	88
Vat reclaimed in this period on purchases and other inputs (including acquisitions from the EC)	4	384	87
Net VAT to be paid to Customs or reclaimed by you (Difference between boxes 3 and 4)	5	3294	01
Total value of sales and all other outputs excluding any VAT. Include your box 8 figure	6	4200	00
Total value of purchases and all other inputs excluding any VAT. Include your box 9 figure	7	1037	00
Total value of all supplies of goods and related services, excluding any VAT, to other EC Member States	8		00
Total value of all acquisitions of goods and related services, excluding any VAT, to other from other EC Member States	9		00

VAT is normally billed on an invoiced basis. In other words, you are liable to pay it from the date on which you raised an invoice, rather than from the time when the invoice is paid. This can lead to cash flow problems. You can apply to account for VAT on a "cash received" basis. This means that VAT is only due when you have received the money. For small traders this is a far more attractive option. Not only does it ease cash flow, but also, should you have a bad debt, you do not need to wait a year to be able to reclaim the VAT paid on your invoice. HM Customs and Excise are far more approachable about this method of accounting than they used to be, and most small traders should be able to opt for cash accounting. Though you used to have to specifically request cash received status, it is now allowed for small businesses and you no longer have to apply to Customs and Excise to do your return on that basis.

6.8 Self-assessment

From the tax year ending in April 1997, the Inland Revenue have introduced self-assessment of income tax. This means that you will have to file a tax return. The return — which was meant to make things simple — is pretty complicated. Though we are assured that it is done to make things simple to understand, I would certainly dispute that. It is unclear exactly where you have to fill in some of the data — and the terminology on this form is different from, for example, the CT61 (there's no mention of "franked payments").

The Inland Revenue have produced a simple little computer program which you can get free of charge by phoning their order line — shown on your self-assessment papers. This makes filling and filing the return fairly easy. The key dates for self-assessment are 30th September — by which you should return the forms if you want the Inland Revenue to calculate your tax — and 31st January — by which you should return the form if you are calculating your own tax. If you miss these dates, you will be charged penalties and interest.

Apart from the general information about yourself, there are a series of figures which should be filled in. The form and the self-assessment software use a numbering system, so I shall summarise the questions which you are likely to need to answer in Table 6.3.

Table 6.3: Self-assessment questions

Question number	Details needed
1.8	Your pre-tax salary
1.11	The tax which has been deducted
1.23	Total expenses paid to you (see 6.11, *Expenses*)
1.32–1.35	Expenses incurred in doing your job
10.2–10.4	Any interest earned on bank accounts
10.15–10.17	Dividends paid and ACT paid, called *Tax Credit*; the Franked Payment is called *Dividend/distributed plus credit*

You may fill in other boxes if you have made pensions payments or have other forms of savings income. The end result is a form from which you (or the program) can calculate your tax liability. If any over or under-payments have been made these will show up.

Notice that you have to make two entries for expenses paid to you. This is because, in theory, expenses might have been reimbursed which were not strictly due. In that case the figure shown in 1.23 and the sum of 1.32–1.35 would not balance.

6.9 Claiming expenses against tax

The biggest perceived advantage of running a company is that you should be able to offset a number of your expenses against tax. However, in practice very little is allowable that would not be allowable on your own account. This offset is done largely by buying goods from company money. You do not personally pay less income tax — what you actually do is to pay yourself less money, but buy necessary goods with the company cheque book, or buy them yourself, and then reclaim their costs as expenses from the company.

Naturally the government is not a benevolent institution, and will require that items bought by the company constitute "legitimate business expenses". for instance, your wife or girlfriend's designer label dress or boyfriend's subscription to Esquire magazine is unlikely to be accepted as a reasonable and necessary company expense. However, there is a significant list of items which can be purchased by the company. Once again, the best advice on precisely what can and cannot be claimed should be sought from your accountant.

Cars

The company car is becoming a less attractive perk these days. The Chancellor keeps tightening up the tax payable on the perceived value of a company car to the individual, and, though it is still a popular method of reducing income tax, you should take advice on whether it is effective for you. The industry still tends to view contractors as flash harries shooting around in new Porsches, with some justification. However, the benefit is being steadily eroded, and will soon become nil. There are schemes available, the most effective at present for companies being leasing. The reason is that, since the company does not actually own the car, its cost is entirely deductible. It may not claim the full purchase price against Corporation Tax, if the car is purchased, since it becomes a company asset. A number of companies now specialise in leasing cars to contractors, and will advise on the most tax-effective scheme of the moment. They will normally require a director's guarantee to lease cars to contract staff, through their own companies.

If you are linking your car purchase to your company, make sure that you have the correct insurance. Many car insurance policies specifically exclude business use. It is very unwise to ignore such restrictions, since, if you do, you may find yourself liable to the whole cost of any accident you have — including third party costs.

I have nearly always bought second hand cars, because of the amount of depreciation which occurs as you drive away a new car. This is a matter of taste, but, if you are just starting out, you may well do a far better deal on a relatively new second hand car than on a brand new machine.

Telephones, stationery and supplies

As long as you can show that the telephone is both necessary to, and largely used in conjunction with your business, you can pay for it via your company. The Inland Revenue will, however, ask questions if the majority of your work is not done from home. For the average contractor, part of the cost of the telephone may be claimed.

When you install a telephone line, a handset is normally supplied with it, for which you pay a quarterly fee. This is not a very cost-effective way to own a telephone. You should consider buying yourself a handset instead — it will pay for itself very quickly. I use a digital portable handset in my office, which means that I can take calls anywhere in the house, even in the bath, where I make sure I lie absolutely still so that my clients will not realise where I am! No, I am not serious — but it is useful to be able to carry the phone around with you.

If you have a business line, you can legitimately claim that every call made on that line, and all its cost, should be borne by the company. However, business lines are more expensive than private, and, unless you are doing enormous amounts of business, you are unlikely to justify that cost, so will probably use a private line. Here you run into some irritating problems. According to the DSS (during a visit), the cost of business related calls can be claimed, but, if the line is in your own name, its rental costs cannot. When I questioned this — pointing out that a business line is more expensive than a private one, I was told that that was the rule. The costs of fax line, however, will be accepted in full — because it is certainly considered to represent a business expense. I have three lines: a normal residential line, a second private line which is largely used for business and a fax line. Following this advice, I claim the full costs of owning and using my fax line, and the cost of calls on the second line. This applies to both the VAT costs and the expenses cost. The way I do it is to put an adjustment figure on my expenses — though I pay the bills with a company cheque.

Many contractors now find it convenient and useful to have a portable phone. Choosing the precise tariffs and types is a minefield besides which Windows programming is as easy as snakes and ladders. As long as you can justify it for business purposes, a portable phone is a legitimate expense. However, if the phone is used for private use, you will have to pay tax on its provision. This came in because of a particularly snide little statement in a the budget a few years ago. Norman Lamont gave a nasty little side swipe at "yuppies" annoying him in restaurants with their mobile phones. It was a particularly distasteful little piece of reasoning for a new item of taxation. Despite this, my advice is that you can charge your portable phone to the company as long as that is its only use. If you make any private calls on it, you should re-pay these through your expenses.

The same applies to stationery and supplies. On the whole these can legitimately be reclaimed. Be careful about Christmas Cards, though — unless they bear a greeting from your company!

Machinery/equipment

Office equipment has always been considered a legitimate business expense. As with cars, there are more and less tax-efficient ways to acquire it. So, your computer — used mainly for business letters and accounts — will be allowable. Make sure, though, that you buy a business, rather than a "games" machine, unless you wish to develop and sell games software.

Software, like computers, can be claimed as a business expense. Here again there are tax-efficient ways of buying it. Also, it is unlikely that you will be able to justify the purchase of a Flight Simulator, unless you can show that you have a legitimate business reason.

The treatment of capital purchases by companies is quite unfair. Until the last budget, you could only offset 25 per cent of the cost per annum against tax. This was an absurd situation when it came to the purchase of computers — the typical useable life of which may only be around two years. It was an enlightened Chancellor who recently scrapped this impediment to growth. Small businesses may now write off capital purchases of this type over two years. Incidentally, software is not included in this — you can write off software purchases straight away. Do not try, though, to claim that your latest Dell PC is software rather than hardware — the authorities are unlikely to be fooled.

It is often possible to lease equipment, rather than buying it outright. If you opt for this, you do not have the problem of capital allowances — since the item does not become a company asset. Offset against that advantage is the cost of financing the lease — for which you will pay interest. In many leases, you also pay a large end payment to acquire the equipment. That will not be particularly attractive in the case of computer equipment — which is typically out of date as it leaves the box. Make sure you read the agreement — and are not lumbered with unusable equipment at the end of the lease.

Travelling and Entertaining

Your expenses in travelling between the office and your client's premises will be claimable. Therefore, as long as you can show that you work from home, you can claim travelling expenses. The actual value of these is best discussed with your accountant.

The claiming of travelling expenses can raise something of a dilemma — and this highlights the Inland Revenue's concern about the true legal status of contractors. Only those who can legitimately show that they are travelling from their place of business to a client's offices can re-claim the travelling costs. However, if you have been working on the same contract for some time — and many contracts run into years — you may not be confident that travelling costs should continue to be claimed.

If you do stop claiming, however, the Inland Revenue will be justified in saying that your claim to non-Employee status is in doubt. If you are working for agency, this may be all right. You can let them deal with the problem. They may advise, for instance, claiming for expenses from their offices to the client's. Once again, the best advice is to ask your accountant. However, consider this: are you not entirely justified in claiming for travelling expenses from home? That, after all is your place of business, not the client's offices. Not to adhere to that could really compromise your whole taxable status. Unfortunately, however logical this may seem, the Inland Revenue may not agree.

If you travel by car, you should discuss with your accountant the best way to claim expenses. Some will advise that you claim on a per-mile basis, and pick up all the costs of servicing and running yourself, others that you should let your company pay everything, then claim a far lower mileage allowance, to cover petrol costs. In the latter case, you may also be advised to claim VAT back on the expense. There are standard scale charges which can be applied in this case. Under the "Fixed Profits Car Scheme" you can claim as shown in Table 6.4.

Table 6.4 :
Pence per
mile claimable
for business
mileage

Business mileage	Engine capacity				
	Up to 1000 cc	1001 to 1500 cc	1501 to 2000 cc	Over 2000 cc	Alternative average rate
	(p)	(p)	(p)	(p)	(p)
First 4000 Miles	28	35	45	63	40
Over 4000 Miles	17	20	25	36	22.5

These are the rates you can claim for mileage done on company business using your own car, for which you personally cover the cost. These rates were current as of the 1997/98 tax year. If you make a claim, you can add VAT to it – if you are registered for VAT.

Incidentally, you may want to consider these figures when negotiating with your clients on mileage rates. They should certainly be paying at similar rates if they are paying travelling expenses.

It is unlikely – indeed impossible – that you can make any claim for entertainment expenses. The days of the tax-free expense account are long gone. When companies pay employees' day-time expenses, they are not able to reclaim the cost against corporation tax, unless the claim includes entertainment of foreign visitors.

However, if you need to work overtime, and that involves buying yourself a meal, you can claim for a subsistence payment. If you do this, make sure the reason for the expense is thoroughly documented. Subsistence payments are claimable if you have to work more than 15 miles from your normal office outside hours. So, if you travel to see a client and stay the night, you can claim £5 per night for subsistence, on top of other expenses. Check the figures and rules with your accountant, though. Remember that this does not apply for time spent in your normal place of work – i.e. the client's normal premises if you commute there.

Lastly, accommodation expenses can usually be reclaimed. If you are on contract at a remote site, and need to pay for accommodation, you can reclaim the cost. In practice, this expense will probably have been allowed for in the contract value, anyway. This will only apply if you retain your home address. The nomadic freelancer will find such a claim difficult if he or she cannot point to a home base.

Home office costs

Some advisers advocate making over part of your house to the office. In this way, a proportion of your rates, electricity and gas, and mortgage can be reclaimed. However, there are alarming dangers in this advice. If you work from home, you can certainly justify claiming for the cost of heating and lighting involved in that work. This will be a marginal benefit, but not to be ignored. Do not attempt to claim for all the expense; it does not all arise from your use of the home as an office. A figure of around £1500 will normally be acceptable to the Inland Revenue.

If you decide that you will claim for a portion of the council tax and/or mortgage, you will be giving yourself problems. If you claim council tax, the local authority, should they become aware of it, may conceivably want to reclassify your premises as business premises, and rate you accordingly. Indeed, you may even be refused permission to carry on business at your address, because to do so would involve an illegitimate change of use of the property. This will probably not apply unless you have a separate building for your office. Today, use of the home as an office is becoming far more acceptable — indeed, many enlightened authorities are encouraging the practice to reduce traffic and pollution. It is a good idea to check with your local council if you are in doubt.

Beware though that if you claim for a proportion of the cost of the mortgage, you could be in trouble on two counts. Firstly, if you do not inform your building society of the change, you will be in breach of your mortgage agreement. They may take a dim view of this. Secondly, when you come to sell the property, the Revenue are likely to claim that a proportion of its increase in value should be written into the company's accounts, and therefore taxable. Since the house is the only personal asset available whose increase in value is not taxable, it is foolish to throw that away for short-term gain.

A more difficult problem would arise if your company went bankrupt. This is unlikely, as long as the company is only used for your contracting income. However, many contractors expand their businesses, by moving into stationery sales or some other area. If the company goes bankrupt, you are likely to be ask by the receiver to sell up to pay some of its debts. Indeed, with current property growth rates, you may find that such a sale will pay off all the company's debtors. This is the reason why building societies are often against such arrangements.

If you decide, nevertheless, to write part of your house expenses against your company, be sure to set up a second charge document and do the thing properly — not to do so is almost certain to cause difficulties. Also, be sure to consult, not only your accountant, but a solicitor. Consider also the effect of your business upon your household insurance policy. If you work from home all the time, it can improve your security, and you may be able to obtain a reduction in premium. You should also make sure that your policy covers all the equipment you own — and that you have "all risks" cover for portables.

In practice, the Revenue will normally allow a sum of, perhaps £30 per week without argument, and most accountants will suggest this.

Banking costs

When you run a limited company, you must open a business bank account. This seems iniquitous to me because the bank treats it as an opportunity to extract money which they would not on a personal account, for a level of service which is at best pretty questionable.

A business account will attract charges for "maintenance" and for every entry made. Barclays, for example (and this is not intended to be a criticism of that company, all the other banks work the same way), currently charges 45 pence for automated entries and inter-account transfers, and 64 pence for "standard entries" (i.e. cheques). In addition they charge a £7.50 "maintenance fee" per quarter.

I am quite unable to see how a bank can justify such charges. After all, they have the advantage of the interest on your money (interest is not earned on the chequing account) – and charge interest immediately you go overdrawn. Even if you use a high rate account, they do not pay you the same amount of interest they are earning on your money. On top of that, they sit on money for no justifiable reason. Pay a cheque into your account, and it takes three days at least to "clear". That mysterious process is simply a way for the banks to have money "in limbo" – during which they can lend it out and earn interest for themselves. I do much of my work for a Northern Irish company, and have been told that it takes five or six days to clear such cheques. When I was told that, I gently pointed out that Northern Ireland is actually part of the United Kingdom. Even though that may have come as a surprise to the bank, I could have had as much effect had I explained it to one of their hole-in-the-wall machines.

One way to cover these costs is to run a second interest-bearing account. These have various names – Barclays call theirs a Business Premium Account. When you are accruing money for VAT, income tax or ACT, you should put it into one of these accounts. This can be done over the phone – as can the transferring of money back from the interest-bearing account to your current account when you need to pay your taxes.

I believe that this process should be automatic. The bank should be able to set a specified limit on the amount of money sitting in your current account and automatically transfer it to the interest-bearing account when that limit is exceeded – and vice versa. As a computer programming problem it is elementary. However, when I have asked for such a facility, I have been told it is quite out of the question. So I have to keep on top of the accounts myself. Quite what that "maintenance fee" represents – except a way for the bank to print money – I do not know. I am not criticising one bank or another – they are all the same. Personally, I have had very good service from my own bank, Barclays. On the odd occasion when a mistake has been made, they corrected it promptly. I am just surprised that banks as a whole have not been prevailed upon to provide a more equitable service to those from whose money they make such large profits.

The P11D

At the end of the year, you will be expected to file a P11D for each employee to whom expenses have been paid. This is a form which tells the Inland Revenue how much you have paid in expenses. At the same time, you should write a letter to the Inland Revenue to claim that all these expenses were incurred in the course of doing business. This letter is known as an "S198" claim. It will take the form shown in Figure 6.5.

Figure 6.5: Section 198 letter

H.M. Inspector of Taxes
Frogsbourne 3
Government Buildings
Frogsham
FRO GGY

28th April, 1998.

Dear Sir,

Your Ref: XXX/XXXXXX YY YY YYYY Y

I hereby claim under section 198 of the Income and Corporation Taxes Act 1988 that the following expenses were incurred by me wholly, exclusively and necessarily in the performance of my duties as a director of Spawning Systems Limited during the year ended 5th April, 1998:

	£
Travelling and subsistence	11,879
Computer supplies	529

Yours faithfully,

Freddy Frog

This letter — and the preparation of the P11D should, at the least, be checked by your accountant. The figures on the letter are included on your self-assessment form (Questions 1.23 and 1.32 - 1.35). If you do not make a Section 198 declaration, the Inland Revenue will be entitled to claim that all the expenses paid to you should be taxable.

6.10 Where to put your money

The purpose of all your work is to make money. If you are new to contracting, the chances are that you will be making substantially more than you did as a full-time employee. This money ought not to be spent as it is earned, because some will be needed as a contingency reserve, and some accrued for future tax. Therefore it should be put where it can be most useful. In this section, I am addressing money which you have been paid by your company.

The main reason for saving is to provide for the future. That may be the immediate future — to live between contracts — or the longer term. If you have been accustomed to relying on your employer to provide you with a pension, you must now make your own provisions in one way or another. Savings must be of two sorts — short-term and easy to realise in an emergency, and longer term for the future. Ideally the latter should be locked up in some way to save you from the temptation to use them to buy that new car or holiday.

Banks and building societies

Banks in the UK are undergoing a lot of criticism. I have already explained the way they hold money in current accounts without paying much interest — but usually charge like a wounded rhino as soon as you tip into overdraft. They charge business users at most exorbitant rates, yet provide a poor level of service. When interest rates are high, they earn a lot more from non-interest bearing accounts which they hold than they pay in increased amounts to investors. Is it a coincidence that the time to clear a cheque seems to have increased from three to six days in the last couple of years?

This is not the time it takes for an incoming cheque to appear on your statement. After that, for some unspecified time, it will remain as an "uncleared effect", unseen by all but the bank computers. If you happen to draw out money during that period you can tip into overdraft without even a whisper on your statement. Interesting little practice, that — good business for the bankers, not so good for their clients.

Interest-bearing accounts are now available for personal accounts, and it is sensible to shop around for the best deal. For instance, most building societies now provide a full banking service, plus attractive rates of interest on current accounts. If you run multiple accounts, it is wise to spread them around. If one institution gives you a hard time, it is then easy to transfer to another.

Nevertheless, a bank current account is a necessary evil. You need some sort of account for bill paying and general expenditure. It should be used only for liquid funds.

Banks offer deposit accounts for more substantial and longer term sums. Generally these are unsuitable for investment of large amounts of money, because the rates of interest are rather low.

Building Societies generally offer rather better rates than banks. However, for large sums they are no more suitable than Banks.

Business accounts, as has been explained earlier, are in a different category. Banks charge for every entry in a current account, and provide no interest. To offset this, you should try to run a deposit account alongside, to earn interest on your money. A minority of banks will automatically transfer money from account to account to keep your current account in funds, and your larger sums earning interest, but, probably because it is not in their interest, most banks will not provide such a service. It is up to you to manage your account yourself. This is deplorable, but, in the UK, the norm. Overseas, in Switzerland, the USA — or even Greece — this does not apply. Perhaps one day our own backward banks will catch up.

Property

A house used to be a very good investment, since it attracts no capital taxation if it is the first home. Since contracting income is normally higher than employed income, you may decide to buy a more expensive house, with a larger mortgage. Nowadays, it is not so easy to obtain humungous mortgages, and the attraction of property declined in the early 1990s to the point where it was seen to be a very poor investment indeed. However, we all have to live somewhere, and property values tend to increase over time – though the heady days of Kensington broom closets selling for tens of thousands are probably over.

- Realising the money tied up in a house these days, even though property values are increasing again, can take longer than you can afford to wait. Having some liquid cash invested in banks or building societies will ensure that hard times are covered whilst the longer term sale of a house proceeds.

Second houses used to be attractive. They were more "realisable" than first houses, which meant that, if your fell on harder times, you need not sell and move to a smaller house – you could just sell the second home. However, since property has not been moving as well as in the past, they usually make poor short-term investments. You must ensure that your second house is in an area where resale values will remain strong, and you will probably only see a capital return if you substantially improve the property. There is a capital gains tax liability on profits from second homes at a similar level to the rate of income tax. Nevertheless, the rules governing second properties as a business expense are attractive. If you can show that the property is available for letting for at least twenty weeks in a year, and that it has been let for at least ten, then all the expenditure in upkeep of the house can be offset against your other income. Since you will be operating as a business, the second house can be a very sound investment, even in these hard times. Property prices, of course, limit the scope for such expenditure, and the cost of borrowing will generally be too high to justify the extra tax benefit. However, if you have a windfall, or a nice stack of dosh lying about, a second house can still be a useful investment.

Shares

There can be good profits to be made on stocks and shares, if you understood the principles. However, the Stock Market is little more than a gambling house, and even though shares have recovered since the recession, it is not a game for the faint-hearted. What the crash did was to reduce the number of individual small investors dabbling in the market. Since then, only a few stocks, particularly privatisation issues, have attracted the small investor.

At the time of writing there are new share markets opening up in the old communist countries. Though these are not yet mature, there is certainly money to be made – and lost.

There are now some very good ways to see the progress of shares. Microsoft Investor is the most obvious, found at http://investor@msn.com. This enables you to see the value of individual shares and to track the value of your portfolio. If you are so minded, this can be a lot of fun. However, remember that you are, in effect, gambling – you may well lose money.

This is a specialised area, and you need to have the right sort of mind to understand it. If you do have the expertise, you can make a lot of money. This sort of investment also takes a lot of time, and needs a good understanding of the principles.

Antiques/motor cars

There can be good profits from buying genuine rarities. Objets d'art or motor cars are items which the Revenue will be unlikely to notice when they are sold – unless the profits are massive indeed. However, if you do make a gain on the sale of such an item, you should declare it. Remember that such a profit is a capital gain, and that you can make, currently, up to £6,000 per annum before you are liable to capital gains tax. You may also be able to divide the gain between yourself and your partner to take advantage of his or her allowance as well. If you do make such a gain, remember to tell your accountant.

Classic cars were particularly attractive at one time, but that bubble, like many others has burst, leaving many with expensive white elephants. The market is improving—but, like many "get rich quick" markets, is very fickle. One advantage if you do buy right is that certain classic cars can be used every day and still retain or increase in value. Their running expenses can then be met through company pre-tax money. However, you really need to love old cars, with all their foibles, and to be prepared to see them off the road for protracted periods when they need replacement of no longer manufactured parts. A sign of their popularity is the number of specialist magazines now available, devoted to the subject. In the more rarefied areas, the whole thing has gone mad. You can even buy shares in a stockpile of cars, being kept for a number of years to appreciate, after which investors will be paid the gain in value. It rather spoils the fun of coping with a breakdown on a rainy night on the M1 in your beloved MGB. On the other hand, perhaps it doesn't.

Another advantage of cars is that you can run a "classic" car as a company vehicle. Since the taxable benefit to you is based on its price when purchased, it will be far lower than an equivalently valued new car. In addition, capital gains tax is not chargeable on the profit made by the car's increase in value. It probably will not be long before this tax loophole is closed, but for now, cars are a fair investment, and can be a lot of fun.

If you are not excited by cars, the purchase of furniture for use in the office can also be attractive. Furniture may be "written off" the company's books in a period of four years, but still be serviceable — and even increasing in value.

Personal equity plans ("PEPs")

Personal equity plans are a way of investing in shares without paying any tax on either dividends or capital gains — indeed you need not even report details of them to the Inland Revenue. Up to £6,000 may currently be invested per year in a general PEP. You can also arrange a single company PEP (i.e. investing in one company) and invest up to £3,000 per annum in that on top of the general PEP investment.

As long as you are over 18, and resident in the UK, you can join a PEP. However, you join as an individual, not a company. If you and your spouse both work, you can both invest in your own separate plans. A PEP has been a very clean way to invest money. There are no penalties from withdrawing money, nor from closing a plan. In other words, you can invest £9,000 per annum, and the government will not take a penny of tax against the gain you may make. (Remember that investments can go down in value, as well as up).

A PEP is administered by a government approved fund manager. Your accountant or financial adviser can put you in touch with one. Alternatively, contact the Inland Revenue at Somerset House in London. Fees are payable for fund administration. There are rules governing the mix of investments, with which the fund manager will be familiar.

It has been announced that PEPs and TESSAs will be replaced in 1999 by a new Individual Savings Scheme (ISA), more details are below.

TESSAs

Tax exempt special savings schemes allow you to invest up to £9,000 over a five-year period in an interest earning fund. Interest is paid tax-free if the capital is left untouched for five years. In the first year you can invest up to £3,000, and in subsequent years, up to £1800. Tessas are available from the major financial institutions (banks and building societies) or via various direct sales companies who advertise in the newspapers. As with PEPs, TESSAs will be replaced by the new ISA in 1999.

ISAs

In early December 1997, Geoffrey Robinson announced the proposed structure of the new scheme which is to replace PEPs and TESSAs. This is not particularly good news if you have a lot of money saved — or if you expected to be able to save a lot tax-free over the next few years. The limit on savings which can be held tax-free is to be £50,000. Originally that was to have applied to money in existing schemes, but the Chancellor relented. The savings limit for the new scheme will be £5,000 per annum. That is the bad news.

The good news is that ISAs should be easier to obtain — it is proposed that they will be sold in supermarkets (the TV announcement had lots of film footage of supermarkets, in case we'd forgotten what they looked like), and that the money held in them will be available instantly without losing benefit of tax relief.

More information will become available over the coming months — but the above seems to be the message so far about ISAs.

Government investment

If you are investing money, you should not ignore the older National Savings schemes. These also pay tax-free interest. They will not set the world alight or make you a fortune, but they are a good safe repository for your money and you can withdraw it easily. The status of these is not likely to change — though the new government may re-jig the whole savings area in the next few years.

6.11 Contingency planning

So far we have considered only the beneficial aspects of contracting. However, there are risks which must be allowed for by setting aside some money. Inevitably, these are more expensive for the contractor than the full-time employee. In this section we consider the more personal items — but your plans should also include some career planning — including self training (see chapter 7).

Health insurance, income protection plan and life cover

When you work for yourself, nobody is going to pay you while you are ill. Therefore you should ensure both that you are back at work as quickly as possible and that your expenses are covered if you are incapacitated for a long time.

The former requires good health insurance. Whatever your politics, it makes sense to minimise time waiting for hospital treatment if this affects your income. The latter will provide an income if you are disabled for a long period. This is, again, a sensible insurance, since you do not have a, hopefully, benevolent employer to help you.

There are a number of schemes. You should consider not only the protection of your own income, but also your partner's. If you are sick, it is important that your dependents are not left destitute — but what if your partner is seriously incapacitated? You may be forced to stop working for a period either to nurse him or her, or to look after your children. Whilst, if you are an employee, you might be treated sympathetically and allowed some paid time off, as a contractor you will not be paid unless you are working. It is therefore important to assess the impact on the household not only of your own impairment, but also of your partner's.

Although you no longer receive income tax allowance against Life Insurance premiums, it is wise to have a reasonable level of cover in case of the extreme emergency. Most income protection plan policies include some measure of life cover. Remember that many jobs include a measure of life cover which will be denied to you as a contractor.

For information on these insurance policies, you should consult your insurance broker — see the section later in this chapter.

General liquidity fund

It is unrealistic to assume that your employment will be constant. Therefore it is wise to set aside some portion of your income to cover the low times, or periods "resting" between contracts. This should be kept in a deposit or building society account so that it can be fairly quickly realised in an emergency, but still earns some interest. The actual level depends upon your experience of finding new contracts. A reasonable figure to start with is enough money to pay for two months' living expenses. During a period between contracts, you can probably turn your hand to temporary work of some sort — part-time secretarial or clerical work or perhaps selling. In practice, most contractors do not need to turn to such tasks because there is just so much work available — and the brief periods between contracts are normally occupied in interviews and negotiations. For that reason, you should make sure that you allow enough money to live whilst negotiations proceed.

This fund can also be used to save money for deliberate time off, such as holidays. Many contractors make conscious efforts to separate out money to pay for holiday costs, and to cover income lost while on holiday.

If you use office equipment, such as computers, be sure to insure it adequately. As a contractor, you may have a sizeable income depending on having such equipment available.

Unless you are paid through a PAYE scheme the time will come when you will be presented with a large tax demand. It is important to make sure that you set aside enough money to pay these future tax bills. Interest on overdue bills is based, iniquitously, on the original sum — even though part of that may be paid off. Therefore, once you are in a position of indebtedness, you find you are sliding down a slippery slope which is very hard to ascend. Believe me, I know.

Pension

Lastly, remember that you do not have eligibility to an employer's pension scheme. Therefore it is very wise to set aside money for this. It is very easy to approach retirement age, and suddenly realise that you have little income expectation.

One of the great advantages of being a contractor is that you do not have to adhere to a rigid retirement policy. Just because you reach 60 or 65, you do not have to retire, but can carry on working. Indeed, many older contractors are people who have been retired from their full time jobs, and have been able to carry on because of the shortage of trained younger people. Personally, I do not really want to retire — maybe just to ease off a little as I get older. Contracting is a very good way to achieve that.

Pensions, though, are a two-edged sword. Some contractors become so enthusiastic that they put aside money which ought to go into a contingency fund. When they have a low period, they find that the money cannot be realised because it is tied into a scheme which will only pay out after they retire. They see a fund of money available on the other side of an impenetrable glass wall.

Personal pension schemes have had some justifiably bad press recently, following the sale of a number of rather dubious policies to employees opting out of company-run schemes. The returns on the new pensions were dreadful, and some of the companies responsible are now having to compensate those whom they persuaded to join them.

It is purely a matter of choice, but I am not convinced that pensions really represent value for money. If you think about it, you are tying up your money with an organisation whose purpose is to make a profit for itself before they make one for you. If you invest money wisely yourself, you can end up better off and with a more flexible fund available for your retirement. However, that is a personal opinion, and, no doubt, quite heretical to a financial adviser.

6.12 Insurance brokers

Many of the contingency items mentioned are best obtained through an insurance broker, or the insurance services department of your bank. Remember thought that an accountant, banker or financial advisor may give you advice but it is seldom impartial (they are almost invariably the recipients of commission from insurance companies). The Financial Services Act has changed the whole market for insurance and investment advice, creating a number of tied companies who only sell the schemes of linked companies. The old independent brokers (now termed "independent financial advisers") are forced to disclose the origin of their commission income, whereas the tied agency is not. This rather anomalous situation has meant that you must now shop around very carefully to get the best deals. A broker is unashamedly making a living out of selling insurance, but will not be charging you directly for his advice.

On the topic of insurance, there are a number of things which you, as a contractor should consider insuring. The first is yourself — in the event of illness. You should ensure that you will have some income if you become seriously ill, because you will not be able to rely on a company's sick pay scheme to help you out. There are many such schemes, about which your broker can advise you.

The second is your equipment — if you have acquired it to help with your work, or to telework. If your client has supplied equipment, it will be responsible for such insurance.

The third is some form of liability insurance. This is not so important unless you have clauses in your contract which allow your client to hold you responsible for loss incurred as a result of your negligence or incompetence. If you are working through an agency, take their advice about this.

As a contractor, you will be buying far more insurance than average. Therefore it will pay a broker to create a good portfolio for you, at advantageous rates. Look for a broker specialising in contract workers. Once you make contact with one, though, be aware that you will be bombarded with constant phone calls and letters trying to part you from your money.

6.13 Credit control

When you run a business, the most important accounting task is credit control. You must ensure that the money comes in regularly and promptly. Companies frequently fail simply because they are owed money which they cannot extract from their debtors. The term "debtors" refers to those who owe you money, people to whom you owe money are called "creditors". A "debtors" or "sales" ledger is equivalent to the American "accounts receivable", the "purchase" or "bought" ledger equates to "accounts payable". The "nominal" or "private" ledger is the equivalent of the "general ledger".

If you are working through an agency, you can expect them to do credit control for you. As long as you send in your timesheets and invoices regularly, you should expect to be paid fortnightly or monthly. If you need to chase the agency for payment, go to another as soon as you can. The larger agencies tend to be more reliable than the smaller in this regard.

If you are working directly, you will have to do your own credit control. That will mean raising and chasing your invoices. It is wise to agree payment terms in writing with the company. You should ask for payment to be made "on invoice" — i.e. with no delays. If the client refuses this, ask yourself whether you really want the contract — late payment could cost you dearly.

If you are dealing with a company whom you do not know, it is wise to ask for references from their suppliers. This will not necessarily guarantee that you will be paid on time, but it will be indicative of their general goodwill. You might also want to restrict the amount of work you do before being paid — perhaps refusing to proceed with a further step in a project until you have been paid for an earlier part. You should not be afraid to chase for payments — if you are embarrassed to ask on your own account (and many of us are), blame your bank manager or accountant. After all, it is quite true — if you go into the red, you will be chased by your bank for payment. If you do use your bank manager as a "bogey man", do not slander him or her — you do not want your client to question why you are dealing with such a heavy-handed bank. Just point out that your bank will be concerned if you do not show a regular income.

6.14 Dealing with disaster

Naturally you will do everything in your power to ensure that you do not fail, and, in truth, if you do things sensibly, you will probably not experience problems. However, the recent recession has taught us that we are not invulnerable — even in our burgeoning industry. There are very many people in the negative-equity trap, and perhaps more who have found that they have over-stretched themselves, and have no escape.

If you do have problems, do remember not to hide them from your family. In the film, The Full Monty, the managerial character got away with pretending to go to work every day even though he had no income. That is not such an unusual situation, and in less fictional circumstances can turn a financial disaster into one affecting the whole relationship. You partner will probably realise there is a problem — and will probably be able to help out as well.

If you do run into difficulties, as a freelancer you are far more vulnerable than you were when employed. You have taken a lot of the responsibility for your personal welfare away from your employer and put it onto yourself. If you become ill, experience difficulties being paid, and pressure from your creditors, you can easily lose focus. Add to that a contract coming to an end with no new work in sight, and you can be tipped over the edge into very serious personal problems, possibly even to bankruptcy. What is more, at that time, just when you really need advice, you will have very little money to spare to buy it.

I write this section with some personal experience of problems which arose because of debts created by the incompetence and mendacity of a partner who left me owing a great deal of money. In dealing with this, I came across fickleness of the legal system, and even a corrupt lawyer (now struck off, but not a great help to me). I found that the professional accountants and lawyers are, on the whole, pretty inexperienced on the processes involved. This added to the weight on my shoulders, and those of people in similar messes. To try to help, what follows is a potted summary of the process.

If you get into debt, you will be harried by your creditors. For small debts (up to £5,000), you may be taken to the small claims court, and a judgment may be obtained against you. You will then be asked to pay up, or make proposals for payment. If the accumulated debts are too high for you to foresee paying off in a short time, one or more of your creditors may petition for your bankruptcy. Before that happens, though, you should be negotiating with them. If you cannot foresee being able to pay them off, you may still save yourself from the ultimate fate by entering into an individual voluntary arrangement ("IVA"). This must be set up by an insolvency practitioner, who will charge you a fee, typically of around £3,000 for the privilege.

With an IVA, you must gain the agreement of 75 per cent or more of your creditors to accept payments on a regular basis to return to them a certain proportion — maybe 20 pence in the pound — of the outstanding debt. The normal term for an IVA is three years, although I have heard of a case where a bank insisted on a five year term, and the victim chose bankruptcy instead. When your practitioner has set up the IVA, you are protected from further demands for those outstanding debts. You will probably find that your credit rating plumbs the depths, but you will not be bankrupt, with the restrictions which that places upon a person.

Alternatively, if you can put together a lump sum (and can show that this is a one-off sum, not just part of you general capital), you may be able to offer that to your creditors in full and final settlement, on the basis that you are never going to be able to find the money by your normal work, and your alternative is bankruptcy, which will probably yield little if anything for your creditors.

If your debts are too high to be met by an IVA — and, remember this is not your choice, but that of your creditors — you may be forced into bankruptcy. You may petition for your own bankruptcy (a debtor's petition), or one or more of your creditors, to whom you owe more than £750, may do it for you (a creditors' petition). If you go to your local county court, you can pick up a package put together by the Insolvency Service to tell you what you must do. Note that a debtor's petition will now cost £270.

An order for bankruptcy is issued by a court. Once this is done, an official receiver, or an insolvency practitioner will be appointed to administer your affairs. You will have to prepare statements of assets, income and expenditure and to hand over all your bank statements and other financial information. As a bankrupt you may not act as a company director or gain credit over £250. You will also be expected to pay any proportion of your income exceeding what is judged necessary for you and your family to live to the receiver. After three years you will automatically be discharged, unless you have been bankrupt before or not done what the official receiver has told you to do. The goods news is that bankruptcy frees you from all your debts — and from the pressure of your creditors.

The Bankruptcy Association has been set up to help people in deep trouble, either on the edge or plummeting to their doom. For a fee of £15 per annum, they can give you practical advice, and the kind of psychological support you need at such a stressful time. Their chief executive is John McQueen. His address is 4 Johnson Close, Abraham Heights, Lancaster, Lancs, LA1 5EU and his phone number is 01482 658701.

Remember that, even if you do fall into bankruptcy, there is still life afterwards. However humiliating and dispiriting it may be, you can get out of it, and continue to work and enjoy life. The worst part of it all, in my experience, is the inability to make plans and move forward. The sooner you address your difficulties and resolve them, the sooner you can regain control of your life.

Even if you do not fall into quite such dire troubles, you can hit difficulties through quite mundane problems. For instance, if you are relying on your car to travel to a contract, what happens if it breaks down? An employee will usually be paid in such an eventuality — unless it happens too often. But a contractor will only be paid when he turns up for work. So a quite minor problem can cost a lot of lost income. It is very sensible to have the sort of breakdown cover that will entitle you to a hire car if yours breaks down.

If an employee has some sort of personal financial problem, he or she will often be helped by an employer by being given a loan against future salary. For instance, if your bank makes a mistake, you may find yourself unable to draw money to pay for your travel to work. As a contractor, you be unlikely to be able to ask for help from your client. This can mean that a simple problem can become serious very quickly. It is useful to make sure that your contingency planning includes the knowledge that you have either credit cards or even an account at a different bank in case you have such a problem.

7 Updating your skills

7.1 Introduction

It has already been pointed out that, as a contractor, you are expected to have certain levels of skill already. You are not being brought in to learn new abilities on the job. From an employer's viewpoint you cost far too much for that.

That does not mean that employers will not allow you any time to learn skills associated with their business, or even an unusual machine type. However, the likelihood is that you will have been brought in specifically because of your knowledge or experience of a particular area. Therefore, it is normally true to say that, when it comes to updating your skills to take account of new technologies, or learn new languages, you are on your own.

Unfortunately, the pace of change in the computing business is so great that more time than ever should be spent by those diligently wishing to keep abreast of developments. Nevertheless, with computers available to everybody at a reasonable price, there are more chances than ever to find out about and experiment with new techniques.

Programming has, in the last few years, become in part more complex, in part simpler. New languages such as Visual Basic and developments of 4GLs like PowerBuilder and Uniface have meant that it is now simpler to develop quite sophisticated systems with pretty fancy user interfaces. However, almost everything is now developed in a Windows or event-driven environment, and that means that "simple" batch programming is no longer so common.

All this has led to a marked change in the skills mix needed to find contracting jobs. Whilst the old favourites, such as CICS programming, are still in demand, there are significantly more openings for staff with knowledge of systems such as Windows, Novell and the PC databases. The most popular language is now C, and its object-oriented offspring, C++, alongside its precocious brother, Visual Basic. Operations jobs are not so common, but there is demand for new skills in PC software and Network support.

The PC revolution is creating new openings all the time. It is also far easier to learn relevant new skills than before. A contractor can now buy a pretty powerful machine, with relevant software, and learn how to use it for about £1,000 – £1,500. Such is the shortage of suitably qualified and competent personnel that the well motivated and able can find employment in completely new areas relatively easily.

There are a number of ways in which you can learn, and this chapter will cover some of these.

Most employees do most of their training on the job. This normally involves some method of learning, as detailed below, and then applying what was taught to a specific project. The bulk of the learning is actually done by practice, rather than theory. It is important for a contractor to realise this.

A contractor will be unlikely to be encouraged by an employer to acquire new skills in this way. Time spent assimilating new techniques, and learning by error, will be expensive time lost. This is why most prospective employers are so specific about the skills needed from a contractor. Unless the employer has some very unusual machinery, languages, techniques or business you are unlikely to receive a lot of on-the-job training initially.

Once you have established yourself as a useful and productive employee, your employer will probably look more favourably on providing training. This applies particularly when, during a contract, new systems or machinery are brought in.

For instance, it is not unusual for a contractor to be brought in to assist in a short-contract feasibility study, to investigate some element of the company's computing requirements. This happened with a contract for a software company. The original brief was merely to look at the system, as an analyst, prior to a rewrite. The intention was to use the same people as had written the original product, to rewrite it in C. The employer, finding that the contractor could contribute rather more than originally envisaged, then extended the contract. The contractor then spent some time on his machine at home, learning C — which was completely new to him. The contract continued, and the contractor showed his employer some work he had done on menu handling. This was merely intended to be a prototype for the system design. The employer liked what he saw. Meanwhile, time was running out. The development team were not delivering on schedule, and the product was in danger of being late for an important deadline. The contractor then offered to try, in his own time, to put together the bones of a system, demonstrating the techniques which he had suggested, but which had been rejected by the development team as not feasible. The net result was that the contractor ended up writing the whole system, and the contract — nearly three years later — is still running. The product in question is, incidentally, on the market and selling at an accelerating rate.

In this case, the company did not actually provide any training. They did encourage the contractor, and they put a great deal of trust in his abilities — to everybody's benefit. However, the contractor was successful, in the main, because he trained himself.

Many employees do not bother to learn new skills while on the job. They are content to go along with their company's direction and ignore developments outside. Even worse, they do not attempt to keep abreast of the marketplace generally. Many mainframe programmers have no idea at all about micros, for instance, considering them irrelevant.

Such attitudes are very dangerous to the contractor. Even when you are in a secure contract you must keep yourself informed about what is going on in computing generally. If you are working on a project on a mainframe, and your company uses micros for data input, find out more about them. Learn the operating system, and capabilities — they will come in useful later. Similarly, if you have been raised on micros, and the company uses them to link into mainframes, take the trouble to find out all you can about the latter — you could transform your potential marketplace.

Contractors should take more trouble than full time employees to bone up on their industry. You should take — and read — the computing press (*Computer Weekly* and *Computing* at minimum). You should buy or subscribe to one or more of the PC magazines, such as *PC Magazine* or *PC Pro*. You should know what is driving your industry, what are the trends and the up and coming technologies, so that you can direct your own training towards them. You must, in short, plan your own career — you cannot expect your employer to do it for you.

However, there are signs that, as employers finally face up to the potential danger to their businesses of the Millennium problem, not only is there a call for oldies like me to re-learn their Cobol, PL/I and pre-AS/400 RPG, but also for the re-training of the new generation of programmers in those old skills. If the pundits are right, this work could occupy all the programmers we have for the next two years, to the detriment of all other projects. However, even at the time of writing in mid-1997, there is still no clear impetus to address the problem. Only recently, I heard a spokesman from the Health Service IT department saying that management had not understood the potential danger, and warned of lives lost and a dozen other calamities. It seems that it might be useful to learn or revise one of the old fogie languages pretty quickly.

7.2 Self-training

If companies will not train you, then you must train yourself. However, time spent training is unpaid time. Moreover, courses cost money. Therefore you must allow for both the cost of lost earning time, and the cost of courses in your contingency planning (see Chapter 6).

However, there is no doubt that training can be the best investment you can make. Another contractor had extensive experience in the batch mainframe field, before joining a PC software house. He decided to go back into contracting after two years. After one contract on a mainframe, he realised that his skills were rather out of date, and that he really needed to learn CICS to maximise his earnings in the mainframe marketplace. He took a gamble against the advice of some of his friends, and paid to go on a course.

The gamble paid off. Within days of finishing the course he had secured a contract at one of the larger mainframe sites, at a very much better rate than before — mainly because of his new-found knowledge of CICS.

The point here was that the contractor not only took the initiative, but that he intelligently surveyed the marketplace to find out which skills were most needed. If he had gone and done a course on, say, DB/2, unless he was aiming for a particular contract which he knew that he had a good chance of landing, he could have wasted not only the money spent on the course, but also the working time lost.

In this case, too, the contractor was not attempting to learn an enormous amount. CICS was new to him, but he had solid programming experience in the mainframe environment. If he had tried to move into a completely new sphere — such as CICS systems programming — where experience is as important as knowledge, he might have had more trouble.

Training courses on your account can be useful. You will probably impress a prospective employer through your diligence and professionalism. However, they must also be relevant, and the skills being taught should be saleable. However, it is not wise to try to take on too much at a time. Choose subjects which are evolutionary from your current knowledge base, rather than revolutionary.

The biggest problem is that training courses cost a lot of money. Apart from losing money by not being at work, you will have to pay from £250 to over £1,000 for a suitable course. If that training is purely taken on the off-chance that you might use what you learn to find a future contract, you will be taking an expensive gamble. Nevertheless, surveys show that 60 per cent of people who pay for their own training are contractors.

Books

There are almost too many computer books on the market. If you go into a big store, like Foyles or Dillons in London, you find the computer books spilling over into the other sections at an increasing rate. You can also find such books in public libraries — though they may not be completely up to date.

From the contractor's point of view this provides an enormous pool of knowledge which can be tapped at a premium cost. As with training courses, it is sensible to look at subjects which will increase your saleability, but which do not involve a radical move from your current experience.

Choosing which books to buy from the plethora available on almost any subject is hard. All the computer magazines publish book reviews, and those of us who actually do these try hard to be objective in our assessments, as well as identifying a likely target audience. However, at best, such reviews can only point you in a direction.

You should look for books which are going to be relatively easy to read. That does not mean that they should be trivial and full of pictures. However, they should be well spaced out, and organised in a way which will make their reading easy. Teaching books need to have plenty of examples, and exercises so that you can assess your progress. The main problem with books is that employers will not be as impressed with theoretical knowledge as with practical experience. Training courses usually provide "hands on" experience of some kind, which books do not.

However, books do provide two things. Firstly they give a good general introduction to a new subject — better than courses because they can be consumed at your own pace, and the relevant parts can receive more attention that those which are not so important to you. Secondly, they can help you to go into far more depth on subjects which have already been introduced via a training course. For instance, having gone on a C course, you will probably be given a copy of the language's originators, Kernighan and Ritchie's definitive book on C. This is an excellent way to build on the introduction to the language given in the course.

As a contractor you should ensure that you have a good library of relevant books. This will enable you both to update your current skills, and "mug up" on discarded parts of your experience.

Books are a relatively cheap training medium — although they may carry a high price tag, they can be read in spare time. Expect to pay between £8 and £50 for a useful book.

Most modern PC texts also include CDs or diskettes with examples on them. These make them very good self-help texts.

Home PCs

Having a PC at home is now essential. I will say that now. Everybody in the computer business should have one, since nearly all the movement in the computer market is at this end of things. The minimum specification nowadays is a Pentium or Pentium Pro based machine, with 32 Mb of RAM, a CD drive and modem, Windows 95 — or its successor — and whatever development tools you need. If you are using C++, you will need a large hard disk drive (at least 2 Gigabytes, and preferably 4 or 5). Version 5 of that product, in its entirety occupies 635 Mb of disk space (up from an already amazing 453 Mb for version 2)! Indeed, all Microsoft software is now "bloatware" — occupying vast amounts of disk space. A machine to be used for serious development will soon need a brain the size of the planet to fit everything in.

Software is also important. If you are seriously looking to set yourself up as a developer, you should consider a Microsoft Developer Network (MSDN) licence. For £1,015 (in 1997) you can buy a year's subscription to virtually all Microsoft's software – all versions of Windows, all language compilers, all Office and Back Office components, including SQL Server and all documentation on CD-ROM. You even get every one of these in each language in which it is available. There are few better ways in which to equip yourself. The cost of buying all these components separately – or even the most commonly needed subsets – would far exceed this price.

Those who are not programmers can also learn a lot from their PCs. For instance, analysts who want to learn about databases can buy good packages for reasonable prices, and discover a great deal about practical data design. There are some very good design tools such as CASE and flowcharting tools available on PCs for an affordable price.

The PC is a great boon. It has heightened awareness of our business, and has also opened up new opportunities. Ownership of one is now essential if you want to project a professional image. Even the production of letters and c.v.s needs to be done in a thoroughly stylish way, using a modern word processing or desktop publishing package and high quality printer.

Internet connections

The other thing which is absolutely invaluable today is the Internet connection. There is little need to keep directories or even journals when everything is present on the Internet. All the main computer papers have Web pages, and these keep up-to-date information on contract availability, allowing you to make direct e-mail contact with the agencies in question. This is an essential part of your contract search.

There are a number of suppliers of Internet services in the UK. The favourites are America On Line (AOL), BT Internet, Compuserve (now merging with America on Line), Demon, Microsoft Network (MSN) and Pipex. I use Compuserve (because I spend some time overseas, and their local coverage is best) and BT Internet (because they offer a fixed fee for unlimited access). Once you have gone into the Web, you will never look back. It is the ideal way to keep on top of the market, and technical developments. Try it out — all the PC consumer magazines issue CDs offering free introductory access.

Other forms of "courseware"

There are many other ways of learning. There are a number of video courses on the market, which, for a far lower price than a full-time course, can give a grounding in a subject. However, they lack the "hands on" experience which full-time courses can provide.

There are also courses which can be run interactively on a PC. These can be used to give you a complete course to obtain, for example, a Microsoft certification.

For example, a company has recently started in the UK called Traineeze. This supplies a CD-ROM with a large number of courses on board. To access these, you buy training credits over the phone from the supplier. This system means that you have easy access to a large number of courses and can pick the most suitable for your needs. The initial version of the CD has about 150 courses which are sadly deficient in usefulness to an experienced person (there's no C++ course, and the "advanced" Windows course covers a "Hello World" program and the creation of a dialog box). However, the concept will attract contractors, and the courseware should improve. It is not cheap, at £30 per hour for "technical" courses, but the content is pretty good.

There are many courses available now in a similar vein. The best source for PC-based courses is one of the PC magazines such as *PC Magazine* or *PC-PRO*.

7.3 Formal courses

There are many courses on the market now for the serious student which, though expensive, will give you a good grounding in the more complex disciplines being introduced. Perhaps more than ever, these are worth considering. If you are moving to Windows and C++, the learning curve is so very steep that the only way up it may be to pay for formal tuition. It is expensive for an individual, but the gains could be enormous — and without such knowledge your career could be shortened.

Formal courses can be found advertised in the computer press, or via the Web (just go into your search engine and look for "Computer training courses".

7.4 Microsoft qualifications

Microsoft is now the leading player driving the development environment. Knowledge of their software is essential to anybody in this business. They have instituted a formal qualifications programme, with exams which earn certification for those who pass. For a newcomer into the world of contracting these should certainly be considered. An accreditation ought, if not actually to open, certainly to unfasten the doors of potential clients. However, a cynic might say (and I suppose I am one) that there is currently so much work around that it could be a bit of a waste of money to get the training to pass these exams if you already have a sufficiently credible c.v.

It is argued that the whole Microsoft software realm is changing so quickly and becoming so complex that the only way you can keep up is by obtaining a suitable qualification. The other side of the coin is that you may find that things are changing too rapidly to keep up by such formal means. For example, as Java and ActiveX become more widespread, you may feel that you need to be qualified in their use — but what will happen when they are superseded by the next technology? (Remember that few would have expected two years ago that the whole Windows Desktop would be driven like an Internet document. That is what will happen with Windows NT 5 and 98.)

Microsoft's formal qualifications — particularly in the area of NT support — will become increasingly important for some jobs, such as support technicians. NT is claimed to be the most complex operating system ever written, and its support is a non-trivial task. The Microsoft examinations are far from simple, and many employers may see them as a more telling qualification than a degree or unconnected educational achievement.

To find out more about Microsoft Training — or any other aspect of the company, visit their Website (http://www.microsoft.com).

7.5 Lying about ability

There are some times when it just seems impossible to be accepted. You may be perfectly capable of doing a job, with sufficient personal experience to know that you will learn the necessary skills without prejudicing the employer's targets, or costing him any extra money. Nevertheless, you just find that they will not accept you.

For example, C under different versions of Unix is remarkably similar. If you are a C programmer, you may be tempted to say you can use it on any Unix box. But there are so many operating environment variants, and so many CPU types, that this can be dangerous. If you cannot find out how to make a program compile, or cannot make a particular editor work ("vi" is, amazingly, still the most common standard editor on Unix boxes), you may never be able to write that clever bit of code on an unfamiliar machine.

Even if employers ought to consider retraining programmers for jobs on other machinery, the reality is that they seldom will, so it is extremely foolish, even in this case, to invent experience.

An even bigger lie is to claim that, because you know C, you can write C++. That just isn't so. The whole ethos of C++ and Windows programming is so very different from conventional batch-based C coding that you have to learn an enormous amount to become productive. Meanwhile you'd be found out very quickly indeed if you pretended you had those skills when you did not.

Therefore, tempting though it may be, do not lie. However, do not be afraid to sell your abilities. Tell the prospective employer that you will learn the differences on your own time, for instance. Point out the similarities, and your level of skill in the language.

Unfortunately you may be rejected before you even get to an interview. However, if you can see that there is a general requirement for Wang Cobol programmers, get hold of the manuals and learn about the system, or find a friend at a Wang installation, and get some hands on experience. In other words, teach yourself, that way, you may impress a prospective employer enough for him to want to see you.

8 Current outlook for contract staff

8.1 Introduction

Computer Weekly, in the second quarter of 1998, has had more job advertisements than ever before. The boom in IT jobs looks set to continue because of the effects of Millennium projects and the general buoyancy of the economy. It was not always thus. Only a few years ago the market was shrinking, and full-timers were being made redundant. In that recession, many firms found it convenient to employ contractors on short-term contracts rather than keeping full-time staff employed. The contracting marketplace was seen by many as a way to escape from the effects of depressed economy. This applied particularly to "wrinklies" like me — over 40 and, in the eyes of some unenlightened companies, over the hill. Many highly competent managers and senior IT staff have found that contracting is their best bet if they are to avoid permanent unemployment. This was the start of many contractors' careers, and they have never looked back. In bad or good times there have — so far at least — been plenty of jobs around.

From the employers' viewpoint a recession means that the quality of staff on offer has probably never been better. For some reason, which escapes me, whilst it is apparently considered "non-u" to employ older personnel, it is entirely acceptable to bring them in on contract — at a far higher rate than they might enjoy as employees. I can deduce a couple of reasons — that the employer feels that a permanent employee wants a career path, and he can no longer offer that to older people if he wants to retain younger members of staff, and that a young "whizz-kid" manager might find that his lack of knowledge is too easily exposed by a more experienced older person. That's pretty daft reasoning. After all, the older employees are probably more loyal than the younger, and more settled. That in itself makes them more likely to repay an investment in their training than their younger job-hopping companions. Still, who said that employers were rational or sensible in their decision making?

So the recession of the early 1990s is well and truly over. It is now widely accepted that we are in a boom, and the overall jobless total has (in late 1997) been falling continuously for nearly two years. You can very accurately correlate the weight of the computer papers with the state of the jobs market. On top of that, we see the need for more of the older skills which were considered to be out of date.

The other substantial change in the market has been led by technology. Eight years ago, when the first edition was written, the mainframe still provided a good source of jobs, the mini was still powering ahead, and Wang was still solvent. Now the mainframe — although still a source of contract jobs — is seen more and more as a sideline. IBM has chalked up huge losses, and Wang has virtually ceased to exist, except as a "me too" OEM supplier. Apart from IBM's still highly popular AS/400 and DEC's VAX, the mini has virtually disappeared — to be replaced by the more wide-ranging open systems box, typically running a variant of Unix. The micro, which was limited in scope to providing office processing, is now asserting its dominance. Indeed, the kind of power now available on a desktop has made the term quite meaningless. The PC now means a machine which usually has the capacity exceeding that of the large minis eight years ago. Still, never mind, software suppliers are still doing their valiant best to soak up all that extra power. Have you tried to run Windows 95 on an 8 Megabyte laptop? No? You'd better be prepared to drink tea and drum your fingers a lot.

All this has led to a marked change in the skills mix needed to find contracting jobs. Whilst the old favourites, such as CICS programming, are still in demand, there are significantly more openings for staff with knowledge of systems such as Windows, Novell and the PC databases. The most popular language is now

'C++', the object-oriented offspring, of C. Indeed, the rise and rise of Windows as the dominant operating interface has made that language one of the most sought-after skill, showing a 50 per cent increase in numbers of vacancies between 1997 and 1998. Windows is such a pig to program that you really have to have something like C++ and all those wizards to get any productivity at all out of it. Operations jobs are largely disappearing, to be replaced by such jobs as PC software and Network support. The latter is another area of enormous growth, which will increase as the trend to workgroup computing becomes a flood with Windows 95 and NT.

Opportunities

Opportunities are there. Now that the PC is coming of age, there is very much more work around, and it is far easier to learn relevant new skills than before. A contractor can now buy a pretty powerful machine, with relevant software, and learn how to use it for about £1,000–£1,500. Such is the shortage of suitably qualified and competent personnel that the well motivated and able can find employment in completely new areas relatively easily.

Object-oriented ("OO") programming and design, pioneered by those of us using C++, will become ever more important. This is bringing about a sea change in the way systems are created, which in itself will exacerbate the skills shortage. The strong rumour about Microsoft's next version of Windows, "Cairo", is that it will take this thinking even further. A prudent contractor will be honing his or her OO skills. The less careful could be left by the wayside.

It is hard to generalise on what skills will be required at a particular time. There are perennial needs, such as CICS programmers, but there are more transient requirements. Agencies are reluctant to commit themselves on general vacancy expectations in the future. However, in this chapter, we will summarise a "snapshot" of skills requirements at this time. The data used has come from analysis of job advertisements, individual questioning and combining information from other published surveys on the contract marketplace.

It is also difficult to give information about rates which can be expected. Once upon a time, contract advertisements used to list rates per week for the various jobs advertised. Now, this practice has ceased. Very few agencies, when asked, will give any information on rates which can be expected for the various levels. However, some figures are given in 8.3 Rates, later in this chapter.

The most obvious difference between the advertising of full-time jobs and contracts is that, whereas the former are almost always specific, the latter are nearly always general. So, for a full-time job you can expect to know exactly what is on offer. Salary, job title, company — including normally a profile of their activities — will typically all be described in the advertisement. In contrast, the contract advertisements consist of lists of requirements, seldom even categorised by machine type, with the barest of details about what skills are required. Company-related information is usually not provided — you could, after all, approach the company directly if you knew that they were looking for contractors. Nor, as has been said, are rates shown. Also, although job types are listed, it is often not clear whether an advertisement relates to one or several vacancies for people with the same skills.

8.2 Skills needed

The analysis of available contracts is much less precise than that of full-time availabilities, though, as might be expected, it follows a very similar pattern in the main. However, there are more jobs available for "past sell-by date" skills in the contract marketplace. Trawling through the pages of Freelance Informer, you come across some really wacky requirements, like Data General or Wang skills, which you might have thought would have vanished without trace.

In the previous editions of this book, we published tables comparing requirements for full-time staff with those for contractors. The market is different now. There are more contract jobs around, and they tend to mirror full-time posts far more closely. Therefore we have altered our scorings to rank the contract skills most in demand. These rankings are derived from a study of the contract jobs advertised in 1997/98. They thus form a snapshot of the market at that time.

In Table 8.1, we rank the top language skills needed in the first quarter of 1998. Note that these weightings are bound to be rather distorted by the fact that C and Cobol are used in a far wider range of jobs than the other languages. However the interesting fact which comes out is how important the languages are for developing Windows applications.

Table 8.1:
Programming
skills in order
of demand

Skill	Rank	Numbers on offer
C++	1	10,592
Visual Basic	2	6,943
C	3	6,627
COBOL	4	6,047
RPG400	5	3,799

Whilst there are many mainframe jobs around, we are have seen the focus swinging to the PC and mini end of the marketplace. This will be distorted by Millennium projects, but the trend will not be reversed. The only open question is whether the world will be dominated by Windows/NT or whether Unix will continue to fight it off. The PC market is no longer dominated by DOS — indeed that has faded almost out of sight. Unix and Windows NT are now the predominant operating systems requirements. It is arguable that the experience of latter — because of its complexity and constant evolution, will soon become the most sought after qualification:

Table 8.2:
Operating
systems skills
in order of
demand

Operating System	Rank
Unix	1
Windows NT	2
Windows	3
MVS	4

A few years ago, the market was dominated by CASE tools. Now we see that the only significant products which are in demand are IEF, As/Set and Synon/2. There is also far less call for methodologies like SSADM. However, 4GL development tools such as Oracle Forms and PowerBuilder are in demand, though Uniface also has a niche (though it is one of my personal skills — so I would say that!). In some ways, this does not tell the whole story. SAP is quite a new product, and has been highly successful. As a result, skills in this are very widely sought — and competent people are at a premium. However, the most significant 4GL is still Oracle Forms — which outscores all the others put together:

Table 8.3: 4GLs in order of demand

4GL	Rank
Oracle Forms	1
PowerBuilder	2
Delphi	3
SAP	4
SYNON	5
UNIFACE	6

Products like SAP are now being desired under the generic title "ERP" — Enterprise Resource Planning.

Database requirements are now fairly clear cut. For mainframe applications, DB2 dominates, followed by Oracle. On other platforms, Oracle is in the lead, followed by SQL requirements — probably mainly SQL Server, which is becoming a real player now that Microsoft are positioning themselves as a serious DBMS supplier. The older mainframe DBMS are now fading as their "legacy" data is imported into SQL based systems.

The Table 8.4 shows the mix of database skills requested across the spectrum:

Table 8.4:
DBMS in
order of
demand

DBMS	Rank
Oracle	1
SQL	2
DB2	3
Sybase	4
Access	5
Ingres	6

These figures on their own are just a snapshot of the market in mid 1998. However, there are interesting trends, which can be gleaned from the Computer Weekly quarterly survey in Spring 1998. They show the overall skill requirements in the years 1994 to 1998, and the percentage growth.

These tables show a definite growth in all areas apart from VMS. They also show very graphically the swing towards Windows solutions using C++ and Visual Basic which I have already highlighted. At the same time, Oracle, SQL and DB2 vacancies are increasing, and Sybase and Ingres posts are increasing far more slowly. Indeed, if you consider the general growth indicated by these figures, you could suggest that relative demand for knowledge of these products is actually in decline.

Combining Tables 8.1 to 8.4 with other data, the result in Table 8.5 is obtained. This table also confirms that Cobol and CICS are still well in demand.

8.3 Rates

Next, we come to the vexed question of experience and rates of pay which can be expected for the various jobs on offer. Firstly, let it be said that rates vary considerably from place to place. For instance, in Scotland you can now command almost the highest fees going. Whereas a consultant in London might earn around £250 per day, in Scotland a properly qualified person could earn £300.

Table 8.5:
Changes in
demand over
5 years

Skill	1994 Position	1998 Position	Change
C++	4	1	+3
Unix	1	2	-1
Oracle	5	3	+2
Windows NT		4	
Visual Basic	14	5	+9
C	2	6	-4
Cobol	6	7	-1
SQL	8	8	=
RPG400	7	9	-2
Windows	3	10	-7
CICS	16	11	+5
Novell	12	12	=
DB2	13	13	=
Java		14	
Sybase	11	15	-4
TCP/IP	18	16	+2
PowerBuilder		17	
Office		18	
Object-oriented		19	
LAN	10	20	-10
Access		21	
Ingres	9	22	-13
Lotus Notes		23	
Delphi		24	

It is very hard indeed to get an accurate handle on rates. Whenever you speak to a contract agency you will be given a very equivocal answer. Nobody that I have questioned has been prepared to divulge a rate. In other words, you will have to name your price and hope that you are not either under- or over-selling yourself. It is a really irritating aspect of this business that you cannot easily find out how much you should be paid. Even when agencies promise that they limit their fees to a percentage of what you will be paid, they cannot tell you an average rate. Is this because they negotiate with every client for a separate rate for each contractor? I think not. I think it is because they are unwilling to show the mark-up they have for arranging a contract. This is a very profitable business, if it is done well. An agency can place a person in a long-term contract, then do no more work until it ends. All the time it is running he will be paid month in month out — the longer it runs the more he earns. It is a way to make money while you sleep. Of course, the agency would justifiably say that he has to find the people, and, in a sellers' market that can be difficult. But that does not stop it being hugely profitable when bodies have been placed.

The rates in Table 8.6: *Rates by job type* are averages paid to the contractor — gleaned by individual discussions and market analysis in 1998. Naturally, they will vary by experience and location.

Note that Project Leaders for Millennium projects are currently reported to be in demand at rates way above those shown. Indeed we have recently read a report of a Project Manager who was paid £13,500 per week — good work if you can get it!

Table 8.6:
Rates by
job type

Job	Weekly rate (£)	Experience
Consultant	1000 – 2000	10 + Years
Project Leader	900 – 1500	5 – 10 Years
Systems Analyst	750 – 1200	5 – 8 Years
Analyst Programmer	550 – 1000	5 – 7 Years
Systems Programmer	750 – 1500	5 + Years
Programmer	500 – 1000	2 – 5 Years
Operator	400 – 700	3 + Years

Table 8.7 goes further by analysing rates for certain jobs by region. This is the most difficult of all to compile, and some of the jobs listed come from the very small samples used in the previous editions.

Table 8.7: Rates by region

Job	London/SE	Midlands/SW	NE	NW/Scotland
Consultant	1500	1000	900	1500
Project leader	850	750	700	800
Systems analyst	750	650	600	750
Analyst programmer	650	650	575	600
Systems programmer	1050	750	700	800
Programmer	650	600	500	500
Operator	600	550	500	500

There are also full-time contract possibilities — working directly for an agency as a salaried employee. These permanent staff members can expect to earn the same sort of salaries as they would command on the normal jobs market, but to enjoy some perks, such as provision of a company car. Thus, at current rates, you could command from around £20,000 to £35,000, depending upon experience.

8.4 The future

To say that the computer marketplace will change is to state the blindingly obvious. However much pundits say, the actual path is less easy to see. Many would have us believe that the Internet will dominate our lives, and well it might. But quite how much this will affect the IT industry is less clear. Of course everybody will be using the Internet and Intranets (the latter really being a more functional extension of existing networks), but whether there will be more need for programming than before, or less, nobody can say. I use the word "programming" advisedly. Whatever else happens, the need for competent analysts will continue. The skills they will need in future will, however, be different from those needed in the past.

In this section, we will indulge in a little futurology, and suggest some of the directions the market is already following, and where they will lead. We do not intend to look beyond five years from now.

Microsoft

There is no doubt that Microsoft is the dominating force in the marketplace these days. This may change, if anti-trust moves by such as Sun are successful, but the chances are pretty remote that such a change will happen within my chosen five-year period. If it were to do so, the company could split itself fairly easily around its existing businesses — operating systems, office products and development tools. Such a split would probably not change a great deal of its direction.

Clearly Windows will move to a single version. That has already been forecast by Bill Gates. Windows 98 will be the last version of the line which began with Windows 3 — and supports 16-bit Windows programs. Windows NT 5 is due to be the cornerstone of the future developments. It is a major release —still in a very flaky state — which will establish the look of the operating system for the foreseeable future. Windows NT will be pushed as an enterprise-wide operating system, and will gradually acquire the performance and scaleability to enable it to meet that boast.

Microsoft's Office products will not develop much further in this period. They will be consolidated about their present functionality, and — we hope — the many bugs in them will be fixed. They already use a fairly common VB interface, and will become more Internet integrated.

Microsoft's development platforms are also fairly well established. However, we would expect to see significant improvements in Visual Basic, which has many faults, not least of which is that it is really not in the least object-oriented. It will become far closer in function and support to C++, whilst attempting to retain a simpler more forms-based feel. Microsoft would dearly love that product to become a major development platform, but will need to improve it considerably.

The BackOffice products will develop considerably. SQL Server will finally boast the row locking which its competitors have always had.

It will be made to look more and more object-oriented — though it will not have object-orientation facilities added. Outlook will be the centrepiece of these offerings and become more and more integrated into Microsoft's Internet strategy.

The Internet facilities will become more and more important to Microsoft. The "Desktop" is already becoming more like a browser, and that will continue. Microsoft want you to use the same look and feel for all your software — and that look and feel will be their own.

Java's future is somewhat less clear. If Sun were to win their battles, Microsoft would have to back down and accept that Java was a common language which they would have to support in whatever form the rest of the industry decided. But Microsoft have already moved on with Internet Explorer 4 and ActiveX controls. It seems unlikely that they will be stopped.

IBM

IBM has both less and more influence in the industry than before. Its mainframes still reign supreme, and the AS/400 is the most significant commercial mini left. However, it is no longer able to move the industry in its own direction — witness the OS/2 fiasco. This has meant that it is forced more and more to accept the trends that affect everybody else. Thus we see both MVS and OS/400 sporting Internet links and tying in with Windows/NT. This is good for everybody, because IBM is still by far the largest player, and produces good quality products.

Oracle

As the supreme DBMS supplier, as well as the advocate of network computing, Oracle is very important. However, we would expect to see Oracle becoming less of a force compared to SQL-Server — simply because of Microsoft's monopoly position. As for the network computer, we don't think it will have much impact. It will, if it has any adherents, become bloated until it looks just like any other network connected PC.

The Internet

We have already mentioned the Internet as a major new force. Microsoft wants to own it, but will probably not be allow to. Sun wants it to be an open system — as long as we use their standard Java language. Oracle wants to have everybody using a non-Windows bright terminal, but seem unlikely to persuade us to do more than install diskless workstations on corporate networks. HTML and Super HTML become ever more potent — though the original standard was not particularly clever.

Though it is slightly depressing to realise that the majority of those surfing the Internet are still looking for naked women, there is no doubting the potential of this new medium, nor the amount of work which will be available for those with the requisite skills. Nobody in the industry can afford to ignore it.

8.5 The future of contracting

This is the reason for this analysis. What skills should you have, and where should you be developing your career? Well, it would be easy simply to say that the industry is so buoyant that almost anything you do will be relevant, but we believe that contractors should also look to their future careers. Once the Millennium has passed, the job market will change again. There may well be far less jobs then — as budgets have been exhausted on that extremely expensive problem. It is possible that EMU will come in 2004 — that will certainly generate a large amount of conversion work on older systems. But for the future, we would suggest that the top skills and languages identified in Table 8.5: *Changes in demand* — and those which are rapidly emerging — will be those to have.

We do not expect to see much more teleworking, despite the forecasts. In my experience, not only are employers usually hostile, but also employees find it difficult to work from home. This might not apply so much to self-motivated contractors — and, indeed, there are probably more teleworking contractors than full-timers — but we do not expect to see that many more jobs, if previous trends are anything to go by.

One area in which new skills will be needed is the whole area of the Internet and Intranets. It is vital that contractors know how to use these, and contract work will soon start to be available for such people as page designers and HTML programmers. Those who understand Web security will be particularly in demand, as Internet shopping takes off.

We have not traditionally been a particularly creative bunch — in the graphical sense. User interface design has not been one of the industry's major triumphs. Yet, with most systems now sporting some sort of graphical interface, and with such interfaces becoming ever more slick, it is likely that we will have to learn, acquire or build such skills. For those with such abilities, we would foresee a good future. The combination of an artistic eye with a sound technical knowledge ought to be very marketable.

In short, the market will continue to grow — there will be a downturn after 2000 when the Millennium bug is less relevant, but new opportunities will arise from the new developments which we are already seeing.

9 Contracting away from home

9.1 Introduction

The last table (Table 8.7: *Rates by region*) touched on another attractive aspect of contracting. There are opportunities for contractors all over the country, and abroad. The spread of jobs in the UK follows roughly the same pattern as that of full-time jobs. London and the South East dominates, with the Midlands next, then the North West, then the North East and Scotland. However, there are pockets where skills are especially short. Scotland, for instance, has a massive financial sector in Edinburgh (the second largest financial centre in Europe according to some estimates). As a result, there are opportunities there which are attractive even to Londoners. The rates for consultants in Scotland actually exceed those for similar people in London.

Abroad, the picture is very attractive too. Germany and the United States have many opportunities, particularly for IBM mainframe experts. It used to be said that if all the English systems programmers left Germany, their computer centres would collapse.

There are also opportunities in other EC countries — notably Belgium and Holland, where language is not such a barrier as in France or Italy. Australasia (Australia and New Zealand) also offer many opportunities, as does South Africa. Lastly, the Middle East for years offered fantastic sums to suitable people. Recently, however, these opportunities have tailed off rapidly, and the rates paid are no longer so competitive. If you actually speak a second language, there may be even better opportunities — and contracting certainly offers scope to learn a language.

The best way to find out about foreign opportunities is to find the agencies who deal in the country of your choice, and ask them. However, beware of attractive sounding rates. Normal American, German and Dutch salaries, for instance, are all higher than those in the UK, so your apparently higher contract rate may not look so attractive alongside normal local salaries.

If you do accept a contract away from home, in the UK or abroad, be sure that your living costs are fully covered. If you are not uprooting everything to go away, remember that you must pay to retain your current home as well as your day-to-day expenses in the new place. If you go abroad, be sure that you can afford to travel home at the end of the contract (and during it, if it is of long duration). Such costs should ideally be included in the overall package — particularly where you do not intend to settle.

9.2 Lifestyle changes

It is very tempting to imagine that moving overseas can allow you to earn a huge sum, tax-free, and/or give you a lifestyle unrivalled in this country. Though this can be true, it does not necessarily follow — and you would be unwise to assume that you could solve your problems by moving away from home.

It may seem obvious that, when contemplating moving abroad, you should discuss the matter carefully with any dependants or family. However, it is very easy to be caught in a wave of enthusiasm and not to think of the effect that your decision might have on them.

If you have no immediate family, or partner, you are a prime candidate for work overseas. However, few people have absolutely no relatives. It has been very distressing to watch the reaction of parents and friends to the events in the Middle East at the time of the Gulf War. Single, unattached, sons and daughters were caught up in the conflict, and their relatives nervously watched the news to find out whether they were safe. In some cases the first news came from seeing the back of a head in a bus carrying escapees from Baghdad. The choice of work-place is important if such considerations may apply to you. Therefore, think of your family and friends, even though you may be independent of them.

If you have a partner, you will almost certainly discuss any decision with them. (To avoid appearing sexist by referring to the partner as the female or male, I will use the neuter form, "they"). You may have a very exciting job ahead, but is there work for them. If they are used to working, it would be cruel indeed to take them from that environment and force them to be living at home, out of contact with family and friends. That is a pretty effective way to strain your relationship to breaking point.

If you are male, and contemplating moving to a country where there is less equality for women, such as a Middle Eastern state, remember the effect that this may have on your partner. She may not be allowed to work at all, or to go out unaccompanied (or even to drive a car). The normal mores are suspended — women are often prevented from contact with men outside their own families. She might accept this situation, but you should very carefully investigate attitudes before making any commitment.

If you are female, similar considerations might apply. It is unlikely that you will choose to move to a country where you will have restrictions imposed upon you because of your sex — in the IT industry there are too many opportunities available without that kind of hassle. However, the local attitude may be rather different from that at home, and this can be unsettling for you or your partner. For instance, in America you may find that you are treated as more of an equal than in this country. This might be and is far less severe for you than if you moved with your partner moved to a Muslim country — but could nevertheless strain a relationship badly.

An American friend of mine, who has settled in Germany, reckons that it is wrong to contemplate moving abroad after the age of 40, because by then you are established, and find it harder to accommodate the change. Whether the magic number is accurate or not for you, there is no doubt that, as you grow older, you become less able or willing to change your habits. A move abroad might reinvigorate you, but equally it might leave you feeling very alone and depressed. Your partner, unless completely acquiescing in your decision, may feel even less happy with the move.

If your partner has to make a big upheaval to move with you — leaving a job, a set of friends and family — make sure that they have completely accepted the change, and are as enthusiastic about it as you are. If not, as the novelty wears off, you may find yourself having to buy a single ticket home for them — or having to move back yourself in an unplanned fashion.

9.3 Children

If you have children, the problems are naturally even more complex. If you are paid well enough, you may be able to afford to send them to boarding schools in the UK. Multi-national oil companies, and the armed services, for instance, often provide such services for their staff. However, if you want to keep the family together, you may want to find local schools for the children. You will have to decide whether you want the children to go to a foreign school (in which the only language spoken may be foreign), or to an expatriate school. There are American schools in many countries, but remember that their educational system is different from the British, in style and syllabus. You must ask yourself whether the children will need to return eventually to an English school. Now that we have a national curriculum, and the GCSE syllabus is a two- or three- year program incorporating course work, can your children return and pass the necessary exams? You need to take into account their ages, and the length of stay which you are contemplating. If you intend to stay abroad permanently, this is not a problem — send them to local schools, and make them become natives.

The age of children is important. You might well be very successful in moving toddlers to a foreign language country. They will soon pick up a different language, and probably become bi-lingual. However, after a certain age, things are more difficult. Moving teenagers abroad, if they have little language aptitude, can cause problems in their later lives. Of course, equally it can be a glorious and exciting game, and leave them stimulated in later life — and more able to accept changes than those brought up in a single country.

Above all, remember that your decision does not entirely rest with you. However rosy your own prospects are, you may inadvertently inflict harm on those closest to you if you do not take them fully into account at the outset.

9.4 Finding work

An important way to find an overseas post is via an agency specialising in that country. Although you may be able to find a job without such a contact, it is sensible to use an agency, and rely on their knowledge and experience.

Agencies in the computer business which specialise in overseas jobs tend to work in particular geographical areas. As a result, they will generally have local knowledge and be able to lead you through the minefield of work permits, finding accommodation and so on.

In Europe, because of the short distances involved, and the general mobility of labour, they usually work very much like normal UK-only agencies. If you are going to work in Europe, this may mean that you have to set up your own travel and accommodation arrangements. This might be rather difficult at a distance — particularly if you do not speak the language. Make sure that you know precisely what the agency will or will not do for you.

Agents who arrange jobs further afield generally do more for you. If you are going to America, for instance, you should find that your agency will arrange for you to be met on arrival, and for your accommodation. He, or your prospective employer, should also arrange your visa. In Australia, potential immigrants are weighed by a points sytem to determine their eligibility — based on such factors as education, skills and experience. Australian agencies should help with calculating your points and making sure that a valid visa is in place before you leave your previous job.

If you are emigrating, you will probably be going to a permanent job. you will certainly be paid locally, and expect to become part of the new society. The situation is different if you are moving to a contract position abroad. American contracts, for instance, are often temporary, as are Middle Eastern. The actual contract structure varies. In some cases you will be contracted to a local company, and local laws will apply. Make sure that you understand the implications of such contracts. It is very hard, for instance, to fight American companies, when their contract is written in a certain state, and you are languishing back in England.

Middle Eastern jobs are nearly all on a contract (temporary) basis. Sometimes this means that you will be paid directly in the country, more often that you will receive at least a proportion abroad. Very often you will be paid "second hand" by the agency, in the manner of most English contracts. There are some cautionary tales here.

A contractor was hired in London to go and work in the Middle East. Even at the time of hiring, the agency knew that they were going to the wall, but, with a disregard for common sense, they sent him anyway. Their contract was to receive money from the client, and pass it on, less their commission, to the contractor. Shortly after he arrived, with a wife and young child, the agency gave up the ghost. The contract was cancelled, and he was left without work in the foreign country.

He was lucky, he picked up another job relatively easily, and stayed there long enough to make his move worthwhile. He was naturally very bitter about the agency's actions.

Others, not in the computing field, have been less lucky. They have been deported, even imprisoned, because their work permits, which assumed a particular employer, were deficient.

Going direct with a client may seem a more attractive option. However, make sure that the client knows the ropes. If they have not employed contractors before, they may not know all the work permit requirements in their own country (how many British firms know our regulations?). They might make you a firm offer, only to find that they cannot substantiate it because of bureaucratic problems. Normally the multi-nationals, and those used to moving staff around, like engineering companies, know what has to be done.

9.5 Housing

The most immediate questions when deciding to move overseas are what to do about your current house and where you will live when you get there.

Clearly there are no simple answers, because all cases will differ to some extent. If you intend to return to the UK eventually, you may not want to sell your home before you go. Therefore you need to find a tenant who will keep the house up and pay the expenses while you are away. Finding such tenants involves going to estate agencies, and looking in the papers for "long let" agencies.

There can be problems with tenants. A musician I knew took a job in South Africa. He let his house out before he went, arranging the tenancy privately with some nurses who wanted somewhere to live for about a year.

It was agreed that the nurses could "rotate" — the actual tenants changing as long as the overall rent was still paid. A few months later, a new nurse moved in. She was unhappy with the price (even though it had all been acceptable to the original tenants, and a contract was in force). She decided to take the matter to the rent tribunal of the rather left-wing borough in which the house was situated. They reduced the rent — which they are able to do unilaterally. The owner could not replace the tenants, nor, at that distance, could he do very much to defend his position. He had to accept that now he was receiving less in rental than he was paying on his mortgage and other costs.

In a second case, a university lecturer went to work in America. Although his was a pretty permanent move (he has been there now for eight years), he decided to keep his flat in England as a "bolt hole" in case anything went wrong. He rented the place out through a property company on a yearly basis. He managed to arrange that the house went to university students who would be there only during the academic year. This enabled him to make periodic trips home and stay in the house whilst there.

His problem was that the agency was so far away that it was very difficult to check up what was happening. He had periods when tenants suddenly went missing and he lost money through that, and when they decided to stay during the vacation. He then could not use the house, and had to stay in the USA or with friends in England. Another far more trivial problem was that he left his car for use on his return. It was not the newest of cars. The battery, naturally, was flat when he came to try to start it (always disconnect it if you are leaving the car for any length of time). When he tried to push start the car, he found that the brakes were jammed, and the car would not move. He eventually started the sluggish engine using jump leads to a friend's car. He found that the engine stalled when he tried to drive it, because of the problem with the brakes. Revving the engine hard, he let out the clutch. The brakes freed with a loud bang, and the car moved with a ripping sound as the tyres, which had begun to decompose, left chunks of tread on the garage floor. Though you might say that anybody who left a car in such a way deserves everything he gets, not everybody realises that a car can deteriorate so drastically when it is merely left in a garage.

There is no simple advice to give. If you are not intending to return, it makes sense to sell up and move permanently. If you find this hard, you should ask yourself whether you really do want to go at all. If you are intending the stay to be relatively short, then find a tenant. However, you may still have problems even if you use a letting agency. The best tenants are companies or governments who want to find long-term housing for their seconded staff. You are unlikely to have the sorts of problems which we have described.

Accommodation abroad is also potentially a problem. If you are lucky, the employer will arrange all this for you. However, there have been cases where employers have set people up in expensive hotels to start with, and then done nothing to help them find a more permanent place. The result has been that most of the extra money earned on the assignment has been lost in rent. If your employer is finding you a place to live, make sure that it is signed and sealed before making your move. If he has only found temporary shelter, get his written assurance that he will help to find a more permanent, and cheaper, place in due course.

None of this can help with an unscrupulous employer. A consultant was offered a job in the Middle East. He knew that the company had some difficulties, but was assured that it was quite safe for him to move his whole family out there, nothing would go wrong. As soon as he moved, the company went bankrupt — they had actually known before he even started that this would happen. He was stuck in a foreign country with none of the safety nets you would expect. He made the best of it, found another job, and stayed long enough to benefit from the move. Nevertheless, the affair was very worrying at the time, and he would be reluctant to repeat the experience.

Whether or not you are moving into unfurnished accommodation, you will want to transport some of your personal goods to your new home. This can be an expensive exercise, and also time consuming. There are specialist companies who deal with this kind of removal. Your yellow pages will be the best source, or the embassy of your destination country. Normally transported goods will be insured by the remover — but make sure that such insurance covers all eventualities, and is sufficient to ensure the full replacement of any items lost or damaged in transit.

What typically happens is that the remover puts your belongings into a container, which then travels by sea to your destination. The problem is that you will be parted from your belongings for a minimum of around 6 weeks — and more likely for much longer. Apart from the transit time, there are always customs delays. Unfortunately nobody can guarantee exactly when the things will arrive — they can only make an educated guess. Make sure, therefore, that you do not pack anything which you will need as soon as you arrive. This is much harder than it sounds. If you are going to an unfurnished house or apartment, even the most mundane item (such as a saucepan) will be needed when you arrive. For this reason, you may well need to stay in a hotel or furnished place until your goods arrive.

It is most likely that your overseas appointment will be organised either through a UK base agency, or an employing company. In this case, most of the details will probably be taken into account for you. Make sure, however, that no assumptions — particularly in regard to the time you may need in temporary furnished accommodation — are made which rely on third parties delivering on time. If you are contractually bound after six weeks to go into an unfurnished house or apartment, because that is the time it takes to deliver your own belongings, you may have to buy duplicate items to replace your own until they are delivered late.

9.6 What do you take with you?

There is also a potential problem with pets. The UK seems unique in its quarantine arrangements. Therefore you should not have a problem moving an animal abroad in most cases. However, think about how a pet, used to a temperate climate, will respond to a drastic change (to the tropics, for instance). It may be very cruel to subject it to that — better to find a home for it in England before you leave.

Think too about your return. If you take your beloved moggie away with you and then come back in nine months, the cat will have to spend 6 more months in quarantine before returning to you. Therefore, if your stay is going to be relatively short, leave the pet behind.

You should also think carefully about the non-material goods which you are taking. For instance, is it worth the cost of transporting a car, when a local purchase can be far cheaper. There are some countries, where you should not contemplate going without one. Although the rules are tougher now, many Australians working over here used to buy extremely expensive Jaguars, Mercedes and Porsches which they could sell, even used, for double what they had paid when they returned home.

Electronic and electrical goods can be a problem. What is the local voltage? Mains-powered goods from England run on 230 volts, the American norm is 110. You cannot use them over there without a transformer — and heavy "white" goods are useless over there because the transformer would be too large to drive them.

Televisions and video recorders cause a problem. We use a "PAL" 625 line, 50 frames per second system here. This is common to a lot of Europe (but not France). In New Zealand, South Africa and Australia they use a slightly different system, but your products need to be converted. In America the system is completely different ("NTSC", 525 line and 60 frames per second). It would be pointless to take English TVs and videos there.

Even such things as hi-fi equipment and computers can be a problem. You may think that one amplifier is just like the other, but different standards apply to different markets. For instance, the transformers in UK products are different from those in US products. This is not just to cater for the different voltages, but also for the different frequency (50 Hz in Europe, 60 Hz in the USA). Because of the effect of hysteresis (in simple terms magnetic "resistance"), European transformers will run hotter if used on a different mains frequency. This will potentially reduce the life of your equipment, unless the capability was actually designed in from the start.

All these little details will need to be taken into account — quite apart from the differences in customs and the natural unsettling of your routine. As long as you realise that they are there, you should be able to handle them. But remember that there will be many other problems which you cannot possibly foresee.

9.7 Taxation

I once knew a man who claimed never to pay any tax. He worked in one country after another, had more than one passport (legitimately), and the tax authorities never caught up with him. Unfortunately this will not apply to many of us.

Taxation of overseas earnings can be a rather complex business, beyond the scope of a normal UK accountant. It is necessary to find an expert in the matter who can guide you through the potential minefield before you start. If you are using an agency to find your job, they will almost certainly be able to recommend someone suitable.

Earnings abroad, kept abroad, will only be subject to tax in the UK if you stay away for more than one tax year, and if the country in which you work has not actually taxed the money. Of course, if you are not intending to come home, you will merely be subject (after the expiry of the tax year in which you make the move) to whatever local taxes apply. Similarly, if you stay away over a whole tax year, you are unlikely to be asked to pay any tax in the UK for that year when you finally return. Unfortunately, these matters can be rather complex, and, to some extent, up to the discretion of a tax inspector.

That is why you need an accountant, who will know how to present your case.

There is a problem in establishing that you have actually settled abroad. Naturally, if you sell up and move permanently overseas, and never return, there is no question that you are no longer resident in the UK. However, if you make visits here — particularly business related — or you keep a house or flat (perhaps renting it out), then it could be argued that you are still at least partially resident in this country. In that case, it will be necessary to convince your tax man, either personally or through your accountant, that you are indeed no longer resident in this country. In general terms, you should be able to maintain non-resident status if you stay out of the country for more than six months in any one year, and three months on average over three years, and are paid overseas.

If you officially cease to be resident in the UK during a tax year, you gain some important benefits. The first is that you can now calculate pro-rata any tax already paid on PAYE to gain a rebate. The way this works is that PAYE is actually calculated not on your periodic earnings, but on their pro-rata value over a year. For instance, if you earn £1500 in a month, and have tax-free pay via your tax coding of £4,000 per year, the tax for the month will be based on the notional pro-rata value of £18,000 – £4,000 = £14,000. The yearly tax on that sum will be calculated, and then reduced pro-rata back down to a monthly figure — the amount payable would then be the difference between this figure and what you paid in the year up to that point. This pro-rata system is quite effective in taking into account periodic fluctuations in earnings, and explains why, if you get a raise in the early months of the tax year you are initially more heavily taxed than you would expect.

If you become resident overseas during a tax year, you cease to be due to pay tax in the UK in that year, but your allowance remains in force. As a result you will probably have actually paid too much tax, and can obtain a rebate.

A second benefit of overseas resident status is that you will not be liable to Capital Gains Tax in the UK. If you invest and realise a capital gain while you are abroad, you will not be liable to UK tax. Of course, if you are back in the UK when you realise the gain you will be taxed.

Many countries have "double taxation" arrangements with the UK. What this means is not that you are taxed twice, but that the tax on overseas earnings is paid overseas, and that any UK earnings are taxed in this country — in other words you only pay tax when and where you happen to be at the time.

It is when or if you decide to return to the UK permanently that the fun can start. If this is within a short time (perhaps you decide you do not like the overseas life), you are liable to find that your money earned overseas will all be taxable — particularly if it was paid tax-free (in the Middle East, for instance). If you return after a good period, you will not have a problem except on earnings in the year in which you return, if you repatriate them. Both cases are going to be open to interpretation, and you must obtain professional advice on how best to cope with them.

In short, the taxation of foreign earnings can be quite complex and involved. However, the Inland Revenue are already very over-stretched, and will probably treat you well if you can show that you have used a professional adviser to present your case in a concise way to them which fits in with their requirements. Conversely they will probably spend a lot of effort in getting to the bottom of your affairs if you try to pull the wool over their eyes.

9.8 Checklist

Below is a list of some of the questions which you might want to ask before moving to your chosen country. It is assumed that you have already made your choice, and found a post in the country. It is not comprehensive, and you will certainly find other questions which you will want to add to it. Often the embassy will respond with a standard printed brochure covering the salient points which you will need to know.

- ▶ What is the normal rate of income taxation, and of sales/value added taxation?

- ▶ Is housing readily available for rent? For purchase?

- ▶ Is a work permit required for British citizens?

- ▶ If so, what is the procedure for obtaining such a permit?

- ▶ Are there restrictions on the purchase of property by foreign nationals?

- ▶ Are there restrictions on changing jobs, or locations of jobs by foreign nationals?

- ▶ Please indicate restrictions on driving by foreign nationals.

- ▶ Please indicate any special medical entry requirements (such as inoculations recommended).

- ▶ Please describe your requirements for naturalisation of foreign nationals.

- ▶ Please describe any restrictions on the export of money earned in your country.

- ▶ Are there exit requirements from your country by foreign nationals?

There are a number of books available with help on working overseas — you should consult one of these for more information as part of your research into the possible problems which you may encounter.

10 After contracting

10.1 Introduction

This book has tried to cover aspects of contracting, from setting up in the first place, through preparation of presentation materials, interviews and gaining the first contract to management of your life as a contractor. We have tried to provide some detail of opportunities available, and of the kind of rates which you can expect. We have discussed your relationship with agencies and with your clients, and the actual mechanism for working as a contractor.

Not everybody stays as a contractor for ever, though. At some time, you are likely to want to stretch your wings and fly beyond your current position. As a contractor, you have limited scope for promotion or self-betterment. However, there are real opportunities for which you will be better fitted than the average employee.

10.2 Returning to full-time work

Unfortunately, most employers who interview contractors for full-time posts are sceptical of their commitment to "return to the fold". It is not at all unusual for otherwise immaculate candidates to be rejected because the prospective employer does not really believe that the contractor will not decide after a short time that the freedom to choose and the ability to earn far better money are more worthwhile than the rather doubtful benefits of the average full-time employment.

Contractors do not really help in this either. They tend to be, as a group, more outspoken and confident than average, as well as more independent and less likely to toe an unacceptable company line. Their unwillingness to enter into company politics can make them feel at odds with most British companies — which seem to be riddled with in-fighting. But, I would say that, I, too am a contractor.

Going back to full-time employment, should really only be considered if you are unhappy contracting, if your personal circumstances change (you get married, or have children), or if you are moving to a different area (going into sales, for instance), or a higher level of responsibility. As has already been said, contractors will seldom be given management responsibility without becoming full-time staff.

If your reason for considering contracting in the first place was to find work because you cannot find permanent employment, for instance if you are guilty of the ultimate crime — being over 40 — you are unlikely to be able to move back into the industry which previously rejected you. However, if you want to return to permanent work, contracting can provide you a good temporary base whilst you explore the marketplace.

10.3 Consultancy

A very logical forward step for a contractor is into a consultancy. You are likely to have seen many companies in action, and worked on a variety of projects. You will be used to dealing with clients, in a way unfamiliar to normal employees. You will also know how important and valuable your time is — because you will have been charging by the day for your skills.

How you make the move depends on you. The obvious way is to approach one of the larger firms of consultants. They have a regular intake of staff, and provide excellent basic training in the various techniques involved, with which you may be less familiar. For instance, you may not have much experience of report writing. The biggest advantage of going to such a firm is that they will find the assignments for you.

Unfortunately many consultancies do not recruit from this part of the marketplace, preferring instead to start from graduate recruits who can be moulded to the company image. How they can justify charging the huge fees they demand for "experienced" staff, when they are often providing very raw trainees with no commercial experience worth mentioning must remain between them and their Maker.

Alternatively, if you have sufficient experience and confidence, you may wish to go it alone, or with a small group. However, be aware that the biggest problem you will have is collecting enough work to do. Unless you have a well publicised and original skill the World will not beat a path to your door. Therefore you must be both salesman and consultant. One skill without the other is not enough. You must both sell and deliver the goods to your clients.

Where consultancy differs from contracting is normally in duration of assignment. You may be, in effect, an employed contractor, being "body shopped" out to clients for periods of time. This is so similar to conventional contracting that you may rightly feel that you are really not doing anything different. However, normal consulting assignments are of shorter duration (they have to be, the consultancy may be charging as much as £2,000 per day for your time). You will be expected to go in, on a specific brief, investigate and file a report for the client in a matter of days.

There have been a number of articles lamenting the fact that there are few computer experts with business experience. There are business experts (accountants, bankers, departmental managers) and there are computer experts — but there is a shortage of the latter who really understand what business is about. As a contractor, particularly if you have run your own limited company, and bothered to find out what the accountant is actually talking about, you will have more of those business skills than the average employee. If you have also worked as a systems or business analyst you could find that your skills are much in demand.

Consultancy, then, is a very logical progression from contracting. You may even work up through the hierarchy of contractors, and become a consultant. The break from normal contracting to consultancy in that case will be virtually seamless.

10.4 Using your company

Some contractors find that they enjoy running a business. They have established a company for tax purposes, and they discover a flair for running that which outweighs their other skills.

If you are in this category, there are many potential openings for you. In your own business, for instance, you can consider setting up as an agency, and contracting out other contractors with whom you have contact. There are a number of agencies who have started in this way — often by undercutting the firms who originally placed them.

Alternatively, you may write some software on your home machine, or that of your client. In the latter case, beware of copyright problems. A number of successful software houses have been started on the back of work done for clients in this way.

Your company can become a vehicle for other endeavours. You may diversify, for instance, into distributing PCs and supplies to your clients. Alternatively, you may see a niche for a totally new business. Your experience in dealing with your company stands you in better stead than a full-time employee, who has no practical knowledge of the legal and financial aspects of company law.

Of course all this may be academic. Even though the contracting market has had its ups and downs over the last few years, there are still plenty of openings. If you are competent, and enjoy the life, there seems little reason not to continue in what can be a very rewarding environment. After all, you can always change to a more responsible job next year when the upturn comes, can't you?

10.5 Retirement

When I wrote the first edition of this book, ours was still a very young industry, hardly out of its diapers, dominated by youthful chaps who had barely started shaving. It was often very hard to find full-time work if you were over 35 because the young blades who were in charge decided you were past it. That was often, as has already been explored, a reason for moving into contracting.

Yesterday's spotty youths are now entering middle age, and discovering that, as well as possessing at least as much vitality and ability as before, they also have more experience. So youth is not such a valued commodity any more. At the same time, the contractor of yore is now advancing rapidly towards retirement, and often views the future with trepidation.

It would be easy to say that, if you did everything right – built up a good personal pension, saved your money wisely and prepared yourself properly – you would have no more to fear than the conventional employee. However, life is not often like that. If you earn more than the average, you invariably spend more. All those terrific investments you made (classic cars, houses and so on) in the 1980s are now looking distinctly tarnished. Also, there is something slightly piratical about contracting. Contractors are risk takers, and risk takers are not normally particularly good at planning for the future.

I am not sure what consolation I can offer for such people (and I will be in this state in less than two decades). However, I would suggest to those of you enjoying the good times that you think ahead to the future. Yours need be no more risky a career than the full-time employee. Indeed, you have more control than him or her over your future. If you do things sensibly, you can expect to retire comfortably, probably at a time to suit yourself rather than your employer, and with enough funds to keep a good lifestyle.

What's more, you should have had a lot more fun and seen a lot more variety in your work than the employed. So enjoy today, but don't forget to cater for tomorrow.

| 11 | Conclusion

I conclude this book on a personal note. I have been working in the IT industry (or "DP" as I used to call it before I got all wrinkly) for 27 years. It has been an absolutely fantastic industry for me. Had I been born in a previous generation, I would probably have been forced into clerical or accountancy work — boring, repetitive stuff which I would have hated.

When I started it was all mainframes with less memory than my TV set controller, and everything was batch mode with punched cards (remember those? You're older than you think!). I have had the good fortune to go through most of the jobs — operator, programmer, analyst, project leader, technical support, sales, management and technical writing. Since I have been able to work as a contractor, I have been able to pursue my other interests, singing and writing. I have performed in operas at professional level (with the ENO) without having to sacrifice my career. I have been able, for the last ten years, to work almost exclusively from home — even though I have been working full-time on projects to develop software products which have established companies in their marketplace.

Though there are boring parts to it, IT should not be boring — because it has such variety. You are constantly solving problems, in an ever changing environment. The future looks ever more interesting, as technology continues to evolve at breakneck speed. Each advance widens the scope of possibilities.

My father used to say computing had no future (he was a successful insurance broker — look what's happened to their business in the last few years). He tried to persuade me to go into something more serious, with better prospects. I am glad to say that I resisted his persuasion. My own son has just embarked on his career — in computing ...

and has found that he has the aptitude to make a success even in only the second year of his working life.

The industry evolves, and the number of opportunities increases. It may be that one day a new technology may render everything we do obsolete, but that has not happened yet. Each new advance just opens new doors.

Contracting may not be everybody's cup of tea. It requires a fairly high degree of self-motivation, and discipline. However, if you can cut it, it is a great life, and you can earn quite enough to be very comfortable. I hope this book will help you initially to decide whether to go for it, then to find your way in, then to make a success of it.

I wish you all good fortune.

Index

COMPUTER WEEKLY
PROFESSIONAL SERIES

Information Technology Management

A Practical Guide

KM Hussain
Independent IT Consultant/Freelance technical author
Donna Hussain

The purpose of this book is to help you gain an understanding and appreciation of information resource management for your future role as a manager or user of information technology. You will discover the concepts applicable to the management of information.

'*This is an essential book on IT management*
'COMPUTER WEEKLY

1997   350pp   246 x 189 mm   Paperback   0 7506 2656 9   £35.00

A Hacker's Guide to Project Management

Andrew Johnston
Independent IT Consultant

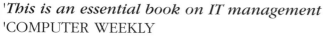

* will enable managers to manage/build better systems on time and within budget
* packed with examples/hints and tips
* contains many Q&A sessions ... indicating common questions and answers found by experienced project managers

'*...a well-structured, pragmatic handbook supported by an intelligently annotated bibliography*.' - PROJECT

1995   200pp   246 x 189 mm   Paperback   0 7506 2230 X   £24.99

EASY ORDERING
Fax: +44 (0)1865 314572
Credit Card Hot Line Tel: +44 (0)1865 888180
E-mail: bhuk.orders@repp.co.uk
Please add P&P at £3 for UK, £6 for Europe and £10 for Rest of World,
and supply full delivery address & phone number with your order.

Butterworth-Heinemann, A Division of Reed Educational & Professional Publishing Limited, Registered Office: 25 Victoria Street, London, SW1H 0EX. Registered in England Number 3099304. VAT Number 663 3472 30. All publication dates, prices and other details are correct at time of going to press but may be subject to change without further notice

COMPUTER WEEKLY
PROFESSIONAL SERIES

Beyond the Mainframe
A Guide to Open Computing Systems

Conor Sexton
Independent consultant, author and lecturer. Director, Trigraph
Software Specialists, Dublin, Ireland

This book provides a complete overview of computer hardware and software
technology, emerging trends and the impact of open systems and client/
server model on the enterprise's business decisions and practices.

0 7506 1902 3   450pp   236 x 156 mm   Paperback   1995   £27.50

PRINCE 2: A Practical Guide
Second Edition

Colin Bentley, Independent IT Consultant

This book:
* relates PRINCE 2 to the practical issues of setting up and running a project
* provides a clear picture of how using PRINCE 2 provides a business-like to
  start a project
* covers the main management concerns about a project

1997   232pp   246 x 189 mm   Paperback   0 7506 3240 2   £24.99

Java Programming: A Practical guide

Neil Fawcett
Terry Ridge, Senior IT analyst Reed Elsevier

This book and CD-ROM will provide you with all the information, data and
knowledge that you need in order to enter into the exciting and ever growing
world of the Java programming language.

1997   450pp   246 x 189 mm   Paperback   0 7506 3344 1   £34.99

EASY ORDERING
Fax: +44 (0)1865 314572
Credit Card Hot Line Tel: +44 (0)1865 888180
E-mail: bhuk.orders@repp.co.uk
Please add P&P at £3 for UK, £6 for Europe and £10 for Rest of World,
and supply full delivery address & phone number with your order.

Butterworth-Heinemann, A Division of Reed Educational & Professional Publishing Limited, Registered Office: 25 Victoria Street, London, SW1H 0EX. Registered in
England Number 3099304. VAT Number 663 3472 30. All publication dates, prices and other details are correct at time of going to press but may be subject to
change without further notice